I WAS STILL ME

RELIABLE AFTERLIFE DETAILS

WILL RIKE

danmahony.com

© 2011

I Was Still Me

Contact: rike@danmahony.com

Acknowledgements

Dear Reader,

First I would like to celebrate all those who have reported their afterlife experience. Each has given a gift to the world.

I want to acknowledge the three Internet archives I sampled: the Near Death Experience Research Foundation (NDERF), especially Jeffrey Long, MD, and Jody Long, JD; the International Association for Near Death Studies (IANDS), Rhonda Bailey and Anneliese Fox; and Scott R.'s completed archive. These archives will receive many awards as time will doubtless reveal the magnitude of their contribution. (I would like to add that, to my knowledge, I have had no contact with anyone associated with these archives.)

And last but not least I thank my wife, Diana Segara, who supported me in so many ways, plus bringing me breakfast each morning, during the research and compilation of this book.

Will Rike
High Desert,
New Mexico

Prologue

This is the first customer review of this book.

1.0 out of 5 stars. Awful. Disjointed, bizarre, and strange. Not well written, basically a list of common experiences,,,,,literally a list. Wish I had not spent the money.

It provides an opportunity to tell you there is a very enjoyable and fascinating read ahead. There is nothing awful, disjointed, bizarre or strange about the reports filed by the many thousands of visitors to the afterlife. They had entirely separate afterlife experiences but still told of similar details (the lists). The result is a new understanding of our very existence. Plus some medicine for the pain of loss—knowledge. And as for my writing, well, I have tried to stay out of the book as much as possible

The following little list is for the above reviewer

*

As to what this is all about, you are in a physical body to learn to care about others, and to acquire knowledge. That is the sum totality of physical life.

Dieing is being born into the real life. We are here to love each other and learn.

Life to me is a big learning experience for all of us, almost like life is high school where you learn all you need to know and when you are finished you graduate to a higher realm which is heaven.

Then I saw this being of light very bright so bright that you could not look at this being. I tried to look but it was much too bright. And this voice said to me, "It's not your time. You have much to learn. Go learn.

The pain is left behind on earth. It does not travel with us, but the lessons we learn from it are eternal.

Preface

1. This book is quite different from all the others on this subject thus far. Instead of providing an afterlife experience of one person, or a few, it is derived from thousands of reports compiled in online archives of death-experience reports. (To make a report an online questionnaire is filled out.)

2. I got the idea to compile a random sample of these archives and chose three: the Near Death Experience Research Foundation (NDERF); the International Association for Near Death Studies (IANDS); and a small archive: Personal Accounts of Near Death Experience.

3. The random sample accomplishes three very good things. First, you find what you find, not what you want to find. The second benefit is that our visitors to the afterlife likely varied widely in (1) their locations: the US most of all, but also some in Europe and South America, and a few in the Middle East and Asia; (2) the years their reports were made (2002-2010); (3) their ages: teen to elder; and (4) very likely they had no contact with one another.

4. As I began reading the reports I soon found that every afterlife experience was different, yet there were often some similar details in one and the next. See <u>Appendix F</u>, p. 355, for surveys of visitors to two national parks. There we see everyone going to the same place, yet their experiences were different though with some similar details. I began compiling lists of excerpts which spoke of similar afterlife details. These are the lists you are about to see.

5. This brings us to the third benefit of a random sample. The 460 reports are of sufficient number to make statistical projections with 95% confidence that the details in the random sample are in the same proportions in the online archives. If, for example, 17 reports in the random sample independently tell of a particular detail, then there are 736 reports (±5%) in the online archives telling of that detail. See <u>Data Chart C</u>, page 350.

6. Hence we come to the general finding of this book.

The fact that hundreds, and even thousands, of afterlife visitors *independently* reported similar details forces us to conclude those details must reliably describe existence after life.

7. Strictly speaking we are not dealing with near-death experiences. The reports are of death experiences, or as we prefer to say, afterlife

experiences. An actual near-death experience would be, for example, a great-grandmother in her last hours surrounded by family, or perhaps a person nearly killed in an accident. They are alive all the while.

The situation is quite different with our visitors. They have died. A few spoke of this fact. During their travels they communicated with persons all of whom were deceased, in some cases their deceased relatives. They were deceased among the deceased.

8. There is no religion behind this work which is essentially one of social science research; but, it agrees with most of the world's religions that there is indeed an afterlife, and I see nothing in it that contradicts religion in general.

9. Each number on a list indicates a different visitor, and a visitor can appear only once on a list. A visitor can appear on more than one list, however. For example, if an excerpt reads, "If I would get through this mission I would be allowed to return home," it would appear both on the Mission list and the Home list.

10. Some punctuation in the excerpts was corrected for easier reading. No words were changed or deleted. When there are multiple dots in an excerpt, an ellipsis of three dots with a space on each side was inserted by me to indicate multiple excerpts from the same report. Any other arrangement of dots is by the visitor.

11. I have used the term *Table of Content* as

this is a book not a suitcase. I have also avoided repeating the title more than 150 times in the verso headers. Instead I treated the versos as I did the rectos for easier navigation through the book. The *List Table* is repeated at the end for the same reason.

12. To see the full report an excerpt is from, as well as the complete random sample, go to:

http://danmahony.com/afterlife.htm

Table of Content

Click/Tap

Data Summaries

List Table

Chapter One

WE CONTINUE TO EXIST

"When I was met by my own entourage of
souls I could clearly see that they were
human."

"I saw my deceased parents, family
members, and friends who had crossed
over."

"I couldn't feel my body—don't
think I had one, but I was still me
with crystal clear thinking."

Consciousness Continued for All. While
consciousness continued for everyone in the
random sample, more than 1,400 reports in the
online archives take note of it.

1. I was conscious of "being me" throughout.

2. I could move around, in short I had an "I."

3. All the time I was also aware of my body and I was watching what was happening to it.

4. I was more alive than I had ever been before.

5. Throughout the period the self-level of consciousness and alertness was there.

6. I felt that my body was separate from my spirit and they were on two different planes of existence.

7. During the experience I seemed to be perfectly lucid and conscious.

8. I had departed from my physical body and was looking at my hospital room from the corner of the ceiling.

9. And I sure was OK, felt great, full of a sensation of fulfillment, and conscious of what had happened to me.

10. I believe I was conscious throughout the whole event.

Full List, p. 133.

Persons Inhabit the Afterlife. After they left their bodies our afterlife visitors continued to be the persons they were in physical life. They continued to be themselves. When they encountered deceased relatives they found them too continuing to be the persons they knew and loved.

A portion of the population of the afterlife

seems to consist of other than persons, however. Our unexpected visitors reported seeing and interacting with entities they called spirits, beings, presences, light-beings, energy-beings, spirit-persons, spirit-guides and orb-persons. Then there were the many religious entities who make up about one-fourth of the reports.

By far, however, persons were the most reported by the visitors. A flip through these pages shows that most of the visitors' experience involved seeing and interacting with persons. The following specifically used the word *person* or *people*.

1. These people were in white robes. [Each number indicates a different visitor.]

2. This person got up and came down the stairs and down the road to me. ... When the person reached me we spoke through thought.

3. When I told the truth I got to go on to the next person.

4. There was someone on my right holding my arm taking me. I could tell that this person KNEW where we were going and it was their mission to bring me.

5. And this person was looking at me and talking and smiling.

6. I had noticed this person from a long way off as he seemed very small, just a silhouette. Then he was in front of me.

7. I didn't see the face of the person I was

walking with, nevertheless he wore a white tunic and I walked on his left.

8. When I was met by my own entourage of souls, I could clearly see that they were human, but in this existence were beings of light. ... I was greeted with a great love and urgency. I was held, and knowledge was imbued into me.

9. I was asked by a person whose image was blurred, "Do you want to return?"

10. On top of the table was a book in front of the person that was directly to my left.

List, p. 145.

Deceased Family and Friends There. Their family members were still themselves, in one case after twenty years. Some visitors reported that their loved ones appeared as they did in their prime. Apparently we will be able to appear to others as favorably as we wish.

1. [Did you meet or see any other beings?] Yes, my grandmother. I did not see her, but I knew it was her for some reason which I cannot explain.

2. I remember my uncle, my aunt, and my grandma and grandpa were waiting for me when I went through the white light.

3. Every member of my family and friends who had died was there. Even my dogs ... Then my brother came over to me and hugged me and smiled and said it wasn't

my time yet.

4. My sister, who had passed away 21 years before my experience, she was doing some type of work with other beings, who had human form, but I do not remember their faces.

5. I remember my Dad sitting on a stoop of sorts with his hand outstretched to me. He was many years younger than he was when he died, and I was just a toddler reaching up to him.

6. My mother, who had died only a short time before this, was explaining to me what was going on and had told me that I was going to be just fine. She said this had to be done so she could properly explain to me what had happened to her. ... She then explained to me that I would not see her for a while, but that she would always be with me.

7. [Did you meet or see any other beings?] Yes. They were at the end of the tunnel. I knew one but I did not see the others clearly. The one I knew was my brother. He told me to do not cry any more for him, that he died because it was his time and that he was taking care of me from that dimension.

8. [Did you hear any unusual sounds or noises?] Yes, steady vector, air sounds like loud jet engines without the hurting effect on my ears, and a voice of people, my dead grandparents, friends, and past historians.

9. Then in a commanding voice, she said, "You must go back now." I turned to look at her. It was my mother. Since her death, I always dreamed of her pale with bed sores and bandages, but this time it was different. ... Mother looked like a beautiful twenty-two-year-old woman with a perfect body.

10. [What was the best and worst part of your experience?] The best was to see my parents and listen to my Father for he talked in a kind voice which made me feel needed and wanted.

11. Two people I never saw before were beaming at me and said they were aunt and uncle. I did not know them.

List, p. 153.

Pets. Six in the sample (approx. 260 in the online archives) spoke of seeing family dogs.

1. I was out cold for a while. It was so strange, I saw myself floating away...down a tunnel with a bright light at the end. Once I hit the bright light, I looked around and I was in a large beautiful field. I saw my childhood dog running.

2. I was outside. It was just this huge big open lawn. Every member of my family and friends who had died was there. Even my dogs.

3. Then I saw above me, my grandfather who had died when I was probably in my

teens. He had a boxer dog on a leash with him which somehow I knew was part of my grandfather's family.

4. My father's voice spoke to me. He said that I was okay, safe, and had a choice. He said that I could come to them or I could stay where I was and continue with my "earthly" life. Each time a beam or glint of light came on or near, my grandfather, grandmother, past partner, friends who had died of AIDS, and dog (a beautiful Bichon) would all shift to block the bright light.

5. The darkness was caused by my family, friends, and a pet...all of whom had died before me. They were hovering over me. I was standing looking up at them above me. Each person/animal moved to create a human chain to block the light from reaching me.

6. In the background, I could dimly see a group of people and animals that looked like other deceased relatives and pets of mine. My dad spoke and said, "Go back, it's not your time yet."

Anonymous Company. More than three thousand visitors said there was someone with them during their afterlife travels. Somehow the companion-helper immediately appeared even after an accident. Sometimes the visitors could see their accompanier, sometimes not, yet usually there was communication between them.

In all cases, the visitors did not know the acompanion-helper, but some said they thought *somehow their companion-helper knew them well.*

1. Suddenly I found myself in darkness where something or someone was drawing me to them, and the closer I got the more comfortable I felt.

2. Through all of this I felt someone next to me. I think it was a woman because it had woman's voice, but she did not speak with her mouth. This woman (?) showed me things. I do not remember all. She said to me, "This is what it will be like when you come here." ... I felt her next to me at all times. She was so calm.

3. He told me that it was not my time to enter into my heavenly home, that I had a mission to fulfill, and my life was going to be very hard.

4. At this point an unknown, but very clear voice, said to me: "No, you're not going to die, it's really not your time yet (with the implication 'you'll live to be very old'), and you're going to get out of this." THE ONLY QUESTION IS: Who is this voice which protects me? Is it ANOTHER (unconscious) me? The spirit of a living person close to me? Or of a deceased loved one? GOD in person?

5. Then I heard a voice directly in my mind. I clearly perceived that it came to me from above-left side. This being I did not perceive

as being "more" than myself. It was more like a "similar" to myself.

6. We rowed back to the shore I had started on, and there was a man standing there. I could not see his face, but he had black hair. He held out his hand, and I took it.

7. This person got up and came down the stairs and down the road to me. ... When the person reached me we spoke through thought.

List, p. 247.

Accompaniers Thought of As Guides. "I asked him who he was and he told me that he was my guide." More than 700 reported being guided or referred to their mysterious companion-helper as a guide. So we will too.

1. The "person" at my side guided me in the other direction.

2. My guide spoke to me through my mind.

3. I was greeted with the most handsome spirit who guided me through this experience.

4. There were various people milling about in grey-hooded robes. One of them came up to me and introduced himself as my guide.

5. A spirit guide told me to breathe deeply.

6. There was another there with me, a guide, who was answering my questions. I knew she was female, and had been in her

twenties when she died, and she was blonde. I knew that she was my guide on this side. ... I believed that I was going to be there forever. I thought, "I'm dead, this is where I will be now." But I felt myself pulled back. No one was more surprised at this than my guide. I believe that she didn't know that I was going back.

7. I felt a presence of my former guide meeting another entity in front of the beings of lights choir stand. They seemed to be having a disagreement about something; I had hoped that it was not about my being here. I couldn't tell exactly what the problem was but I sensed there was a very serious one. I had the sense that I was being brought back to life back on the earthly plane, and that this entity talking to my guide was not happy about this turn of events.

8. I must have given my guide a startled look. He repeats that people, as they take full advantage of all the wonderful SOUL-GROWING programs here, they grow younger in age! And in fact I am told that this center is where one fills out all those dimly awakened dreams of creative longings for growth, but were not done while one was still ... .

9. On my left side, I view people walking two by two in a very calm way. One is a person who crossed; the other is their guide. ...

Guides came for the ones on the left and those on the right were having difficulty.

10. Some were being welcomed with open arms and carefully guided through the transition point and into the wonderful light of the white tunnel.

11. I asked him who he was and he told me that he was my guide.

12. I did talk to a Shaman from the Ojibwa Tribe in Northern Wisconsin and he told me the figure I was following toward the tunnel was my spiritual guide. To this day I believe him.

13. John Beals gave this remarkable account to a friend shortly before his death in 1796. "... A person, clothed in white raiment, drew to his bedside and bade him to arise and follow him. ... John was brought to Heaven by his Guide ..."

14. My guide sat behind the table, and with his index finger pointed in the book, he scanned through the page to see if he found my name on the book.

15. "So much for choice; everything is pre-determined," I thought. "Not so," my guide said. "Almost all of your choices are free.

16. I sensed that my guide disapproved of the non-traditional attire ...

17. [Did you meet or see any other beings?] My guide was the most attractive male I have ever seen.

18. I had spiritual guides who gave me what

I call "a tour of the universe."

Persons with No Apparent Gender.

1. This figure was very tall. I am guessing it was about 8 feet tall or so. I am saying "it" because I could not tell if it was male or female.
2. We are greeted by a "being" that is light, it's like a glow coming from it. I don't know if it's a she or a he.
3. There were three silhouettes. They weren't male or female.
4. A radiant being in long white robes was there to greet me. I could not discern the sex of the being, or the face of the being.
5. I felt as though this person was both male and female.
6. Seemingly, this "being" was made of two beings. There was a sense of it being both male and female, the perfect blending of the two attributes. From now on, I shall refer to them as "they" because that is what they were and are.
7. I could not make out faces as male or female.
8. I will never forget the words spoken to me by neither a male nor female voice that said, "Don't be scared, you're going to be okay."

Light Persons and the Person in the Light.

1. I saw an immense, central light at the end of the path. It was as if a superior being was seated at the end, very luminous. Additionally, he interrogated me about why I was in that place.

2. ... and the warm light was "God" or my idea of God - I felt loved and cared for and precious - which was fabulous ...

3. The light is becoming brighter and larger, and all I can feel is the presence of good, and now am sure this is where I need to be. Finally, the end of the tunnel is here, and I am enveloped in that same light, that without a word spoken, directed me here.

4. I got closer to the light, to the point where the darkness disappeared and I was preparing to join the light. It felt wonderful. Then a loving, caring voice said quite clearly, without words, "It's not your time. You must go back." [Did you see a light?] It was blinding, but out of it radiated the most wondrous feelings of love, peace and joy. I couldn't wait to join it.

5. I saw a figure of light come towards me out of the light. This figure was very tall. I am guessing it was about 8 feet tall or so. I am saying "it" because I could not tell if it was male or female. The "being" spoke to me although the words were not heard with my ears. It was as if someone was speaking in

my head, although it was not my voice I heard. Everything was so crystal clear and seemed to make perfect sense although logically it was impossible. The figure told me "You must go back, we are not ready for you yet."

6. Then a bright light appeared having a soft man's voice ... The light also gave me an important message to follow it as much possible.

7. [Had two nde's.] On both occasions a being of white light appeared to me and took my hand and took me to a door that opened on its own.

List, p. 161.

Orb Persons.

1. I had lost my physical form and became a sphere where I could see all around me at once. It felt like a perfectly natural shape for me.

2. In front of me was something that's hard to describe, almost like an orb or a spirit of some kind. But I heard someone say, "You're not supposed to be here yet. Come with me and go back to your home, it's not your time." I asked, "Am I dead?" The shiny thing approached me and I almost felt as if I were being pulled into the light, which was still far away. As I got closer to the light, everything started getting dark. Soon I was in complete

darkness and felt as if I were falling up and I heard a booming voice say, "I love you but you haven't experienced my gift to you yet. If you were to go now you would never get to see what it is like to..." and I woke up.

3. I looked around and saw very large Pure Love Orbs with silhouettes of human souls - like a chalk outline of a dead body.

4. There are some souls that appear as wispy, cloud-like entities. They take the form of a small ball when they are far away. But, still swirling, leaving a sort of hole in the middle when the ball begins to disperse, then swirls in a circular motion. The ball becomes larger the closer it gets to you. Then when it begins to disperse (with the hole in the middle), the outline takes a human head shape, but eventually disengages to swirl. The process keeps repeating itself, as the soul draws closer to you.

5. I was being pulled into a white Light. I wanted to get there as quickly as possible, because all of these wonderful, ecstatic, feelings emanating from this Light. ... I rushed faster and faster to reach that light. I emerged in a sea of spheres. We were luminous (I had illuminated the tunnel while traveling there.) We could pass through each other, and it was overwhelming the feelings and thought forms I experienced. All of us were trying to get as close as we could to the

location of where all these wonderful feelings were coming from: A HUGE SPHERE that was just as easy to pass through as we were even though I never made it that close. Next thing I knew I was sent shooting back into my body. The paramedics were there, a young male paramedic was wiping my face with a wet towel and telling me to "Breathe."

6. All of a sudden, I heard giggling and laughing. I looked up and across this lake, river, divide, or whatever and saw these three spheres on my far left. They looked like big cotton balls but ethereal, not dense like cotton. They were so excited to see me. I knew it. I sensed it. Everything said was all telepathic as if energy thoughts coming across. Communication was fast. I didn't have to wait or think about it. I just knew. Their laughter and excitement felt so contagious. I just wanted to go over there. It was so drawing. (For example, when you're sitting in a restaurant and the table near you is having such a good time laughing hysterically, you want to find out what's so funny and laugh too.) I was ready to go over and find out what was so funny. They immediately stopped me and said, "No! We'll come to you." In the next immediate second, they were there on my side. They just came in me, all three. They melded into me ...

7. A female voice told me that what I create is mine. I then looked at the direction where

this voice was coming from and I saw her. She was consciousness itself. She was like a huge orb of white light with many hands going in and out of her. She was like billons of conscious minds put together. I was also part of her because I saw white light in a form of an umbilical cord attaching her to me. Then I was being treated as a baby because she was massaging my neck. The love I felt for her was greater than that of any love I have felt in this world. I felt something inside of me, like I did not accomplish a task. I did not remember what it was, but I knew that I had to do it. I remember saying that I have to go back.

8. All around me were beings of pulsing, colored light, and indescribable music/singing full of joy and praise. The beings did not have human shape; they were more like oval or round pulsing loci of light. There were no sharp outlines in this realm; everything seemed to gently blend into everything else a little.

9. The 'many who were there' were without any body-form like we know, they merely looked like little packets or little dull colored balls

10. I seemed to be shrinking to a ball shape centered near my throat.

11. And the light replied, "I will not harm you." These were not words but thoughts which passed between us. Still closer and

brighter the light came. I strained to detect its surface but could not. It was about the size of a beach ball, with no discernible surface. I asked, "Who or What are you?" It replied, "That's not important right now. You are not where it is expected to find anyone." I gave my name and insisted upon reciprocity as a courtesy. And was rebuffed again. The being of light—I lack a better description—began to look through my life. It simply shone into me and scenes from my life projected around me as if I were seeing them again. A lot like looking at a hologram, but full color 3-D with sound and scent. We flitted from scene to scene. Sometimes on fast-forward, sometimes pausing to note some major or minor detail. ... With no movement at all, we were now at a large library. The one who had been doing my life review was no longer a ball of light but now a hooded and robed figure. And still inscrutable.

12. I felt like a lifeless ball speeding down from the sky with force, but the motion was towards the sky.

Few Visitors Wanted to Return to Physical Life. Most often it was the guide who sent them back physical life, and most visitors definitely did not want to come back. It was easier to compile the much shorter list of those who willingly returned.

1. My "pleasure" intensified to the highest degree the further I drew away from life, I realised; and so I wanted to come back.

2. I was going to this island that he pointed at where people were happy and he told me about all the wonderful things there. It was the most wonderful experience. I was filled with so much happiness. Then I started crying. I told him that I did not want to go. I told him that I loved my husband very much, and I did not want to leave him. I also told him that I had a baby and I had other kids, I had to take care of that were just babies. I cried and cried, and begged and begged. He asked me over and over again, "Are you sure?" I told him, "Yes, yes, please, please, please let me go back." It seemed to take a very long time, but, he finally agreed. He told me that going back was going to hurt. He asked if I understood the pain that I would have going back. I told him I didn't care, I wanted to go back. He smiled and said okay, you can go back, I will let you go.

3. Then I heard a voice directly in my mind. I clearly perceived that it came to me from above-left side. This being I did not perceive as being "more" than myself. It was more like a "similar" to myself. A telepathic dialogue took place in which certain questions were asked and I was compelled to answer truthfully. At the end, I made a decision, and at that point the "void"

stopped and, with difficulty, I made it back to the shore.

4. I needed more time, but she gave an insistent order to make my choice and said whatever I choose will be fine. At that time, I turned around, back to the direction I had so calmly came from, and was immediately pulled back through the dark tunnel.

5. Then, I realized my little sister needed me so I had to come back.

6. I had been aware of the tunnel of light with me for a while, but did not seem compelled to approach it. I was allowed to make the decision whether or not to return.

7. Somehow I knew I had to enter the right door in the limited time I had as after that all the doors would close never to open again leaving me all alone in the dark void forever. I also knew that if I entered the wrong door the memories from that stage of my life till today would be erased. I started fearing not death but isolation or never being able to see my two sons & husband again, or even not recognizing them after I wake up. I feel time is slipping out of my hands and I decide that I'd rather enter the wrong door than stay back in my head. I just think of GOD & put my foot forward to enter the speeding doors and at that very moment I feel the anesthetist slapping my cheeks & calling my name.

8. I also remember that my family members

were in the hospital room crying, and I despairing at seeing them suffer. I wanted to return rapidly.

9. Right then I began to pray to god to let me live because I wasn't ready. I just had a baby that May, and had three other small children. They needed me, and I needed them.

10. The presence was telling me I would no longer have any worries or troubles, and was so calming. We got to a white bridge and I was ready to go over when the presence said it was okay to go over but told me I had three small children on this side. So I remained on this side.

11. Then we stopped in front of a door on the left. I don't know what color the door was, all I knew was it was a door and I was not going through it! I kept saying NO! The next thing I remember was my husband telling me I had a seizure.

12. Suddenly I was given a choice. I could go back to earth and back to the human body that I was living in or I could stay in these realms. I wanted to stay forever and stated just that. ... I saw my friend ... struggling to breathe. ... I was concerned about what was going to happen to her. I turned to the Presence and said that I wanted to return and the Presence said I could return but I had to do something. I had to promise before it would let me return. I promised and swore on my heart with all my might. I promised

and promised. The next thing I knew I was back in my body.

13. I had no questions about going with them but asked many about what will be if I decided to stay. Some of my questions were: 1. If I decided to stay will I get better? 2. Will the pain go away? 3. How will I know that all will be ok after I decide to live? 4. Is there something that I am to do on earth and therefore should decide to live? I was given more or less answers to my questions. I knew when they didn't want to answer and left it at that. The moment I made my decision I was back in my body and fell asleep.

14. It was like my inner conscience was talking to me. It asked, "Are you ready to come home?" I knew it meant death. I thought about it, I really did, I thought so hard and for what seemed like hours I contemplated. Do I really want to die? This was the greatest feeling I had ever experienced, do I want this feeling to end? My answer was 'no'. I wanted to live a life. ... Again, the inner conscience 'spoke', and asked "Are you sure?" Again I contemplated for what seemed like hours, now having this new level of understanding. (Could me and my mother really never stay as close as we were? Would I really get the chance to have kids, despite my heart?). I chose 'Yes'.

15. I was given a choice as I was traveling

down this tunnel to live or carry on through the tunnel. ... I felt like it wasn't time yet, so held my husband next to me and started breathing again and felt myself go back down to Earth.

16. [Did you meet or see any other beings?] I felt something or someone was there. It seemed I was given a choice to stay or go back.

17. Then a worry made me turn from where I was. I knew that I would never have been able to return without that worry that made me come back, and I don't know if it was the right thing to come back. In any case it was only in that instant when I returned that I felt the worry. ... I saw my girlfriend yelling, but I couldn't hear her. But that didn't interest me. I was at peace. And I was returning. Without walking and without any sensation of movement I was returning to myself until I reached the surface of my body lying on the seat, until I and my body were reunited perfectly, and then I turned to my girlfriend and said why are you screaming. It was her screaming and her terror and her panic that had created the worry.

18. I was sad thinking about the pain that my death was causing everybody and I said to myself that I needed to go back. It wasn't fair even if the peace and serenity that I was feeling was so wonderful and unexplainable.

I said to myself it doesn't matter if it hurts I have to go back.

19. I thought of my life and fiancée and decided to go back

Love from the Guides. Many said they felt extraordinary love from their guide.

1. I was very sharp and aware, and in the presence of an intelligence that adored me, or so it seemed.

2. I was like a baby wrapped in love. But the love was so intense, I did wonder a little about it I think. It felt new. Like a rebirth.

3. I reached up and touched his beard with my right hand and felt the most immense sense of love and understanding. Until this day this feeling has never left me.

List, p. 281.

Guides Intervene in Physical Life? Consider the following from the book *The Third Man Factor.*

"Accounts of experiencing a supportive presence in extreme situations—sometimes called the 'third-man phenomenon'—are common in mountaineering literature. In 1933, Frank Smythe made it to within 1,000 feet of the summit of Mount Everest before turning around. On the way down, he stopped to eat a mint cake, cutting it in half to share with someone who wasn't there but who had seemed to be his partner all day. On Nanga Parbat, on a 1970 climb during which his brother died, Reinhold Messner recalled being accompanied by a companion who offered wordless comfort and encouragement.

"In '*The Third Man Factor*,' (Viking Canada, 2009) John Geiger, a fellow at the University of Toronto, presents many accounts of such experiences, and not only from climbers. Among those who have felt a ghostly companionship he cites Charles Lindbergh on his solo flight across the Atlantic in 1927 and the last man to walk out of the South Tower of the World Trade Center before it collapsed on 9/11. 'Over the years,' Mr. Geiger writes, 'the experience has occurred again and again, not only to 9/11 survivors, mountaineers, and divers, but also to polar explorers, prisoners of war, solo sailors, shipwreck survivors, aviators, and astronauts. All have escaped traumatic events only to tell strikingly similar stories of having experienced the close presence of a companion and helper.'"— *Wall Street Journal*

The companion-helpers are remarkably similar to the afterlife guides..

1. On my way to work at 3:30am I fell asleep on Highway 59. I remember to be the only car on the road. I do remember thinking about an experience I had around a month before that night when I was driving, I dosed

off for a moment and when I opened my eyes, I seen a dark a black puff of smoke hit my windshield and vanished. After thinking of that, I was almost half way to work. Then the next thing I remember was that I was moving in slow motion across an open field of green grass. And it was a sunny day. Bright and sunny day. (Remember I was on my way to work at 3:30am in the morning. It was pitch dark and no grass.) And as I was driving through the field, all the tree was right in front of me. So I swerved to miss it. Then I was just there watching myself, bent over holding my stomach, asking for help softly. Then from there I was in a man's house, blood all over me, sitting on his chair, saying only, "Help, I hurt." Then from there, all I remember was being in the hospital. I was told after finally waking up after two days that no one knows how I was still alive. That I rolled my vehicle seven times going 60 mph. The car was totaled. And then they told me that I walked a quarter of a mile up the highway to a man's house to get help. But no one knows how since I fractured my spine, broke three ribs, busted open my head and punctured my right lung. Everyone said there was no way I could have walked that far in my condition or even survived the whole accident.

2. I came onto the bridge, lost control of my car, thought I would die, saw my life pass

in front of me. And at that same moment, something intervened to redirect my car and I glided safely to the other side. The next day, I took a walk near the bridge to study the icy effects and discover details. The bridge was closed. Someone else had gone over it after me, lost control and did not survive.

List, p. 289.

Chapter Two

DARK TUNNELS, VOIDS AND PUNISHMENT PLACES

> "It was the worst thing that a person can ever experience. There was suffering, pain, remorse, guilt."

> "I was in a dark void or space like in the universe without the stars."

> "That you go to Hell after being a bad boy/girl is not a fact. It is just a political and religious concept to have you under control. Yes there is a purgatory, but it is not Hell with fire and torture."

The tunnels, voids and punishment places could be considered to be on a spectrum from happiness to hell.

Images of Punishment. First we need to remind ourselves that there can't be any physical pain in the afterlife. A person without a body cannot experience of physical pain.

Intensely negative emotions, however, must be possible for persons without bodies because, as thousands of visitors reported, the intense emotion of love was felt.

> I heard moaning that made me get cold chills down my spine. I looked at the stream that was a bit lower than me which was to my left, and there were dead bodies floating in it.

Of course there can be no actual dead bodies there, just images of them. And in the following example, there can be no physical mud there, but somehow one can be detained by it

> I found myself in a viscous sea of mud. There were a lot of people with me and we were trying to escape from it but could not. ... I then thought that this was HELL, and I thought, "Oh My! This looks like Dante's hell.

Reports of Punishment Places. Let's start with the more than nearly six hundred visitors who used the word "hell" in their reports. Half of them reported directly experiencing a hellish place, while one or two others gave their opinion that there was only a sort of purgatory.

> 1. I was very depressed and barely ate anything for months. I thought that a bottle of sleeping pills would be sufficient to kill

me. I took the pills at a supermarket one block from my house. Within minutes I felt disoriented and wondered if I would make it home. ... I arrived home and went to bed. My world ceased to exist, except for my mind, and an incredible feeling of wrong and unease beyond words. I remained trapped in this condition for an eternity, which seemed like hell for there was no possibility of hope or change, just a timeless eternal agony. Eventually I floated above my body and saw p convulsing on the bed. At some point, I re-entered my body and came back to life.

2. Along the sides of me were other people who were in the darkness that were trying to climb up but couldn't and seemed stuck in a huge mass of themselves. ... Those that had welcomed me were gently moving me back toward the darkness. I was told that in time I would visit again and to be vigilant in my life. I went backward into the darkness and saw the people on either side of me pulling at each other and trying to find the light.

3. I then was in a dark meeting room with doctors sitting around with one standing facilitating over the others with charts and information on my case. I tried to cry out "poison", but to no avail. I was scared and I felt death. My brief encounter continued on, I felt that I was subterranean. For some reason I noted seeing a statue of "The

Thinker", and then it was dark, hot, extremely hot, the surroundings were rocky, dusty, like a canyon underground and I was being led downward with the heat intensifying. I blacked out form there I awakened into a blinding light, the light of the sun, like I said, it was so bright it was blinding, I turned and looked down to see mountains, filled with trees, a valley with a beautiful river flowing, as I turned, I saw the river flow into the ocean, untouched by humans. No bridges, people, utilities, just raw beauty. I felt alive.

4. An unusual NDE occurred during my routine visit to a dentist some years ago. I was at that time a young married woman with school age children. The health professional in question used drugs and hypnosis unethically as a means to induce bizarre traumatic hypnotic scenarios which preceded a `clinical death' and subsequent experience of being deliberately sent to "hell" in an afterlife. This terrible "too real" aspect of the NDE ceased when I invoked the name of God as an appeal for help.

5. That you go to Hell after being a bad boy/girl is not a fact, it is just a political and religious concept to have you under control. Yes there is a purgatory but it is not Hell with fire and torture.

6. After a blow, I found myself in a viscous sea of mud. There were a lot of people with

me and we were trying to escape from it but could not. I was completely desperate; these people were suffering a lot, they were in torment (while I remember this, my skin goes bristled and my body recalls the horrible sensation). I then thought that this was HELL, and I thought, "Oh My! This looks like Dante's hell and also remember thinking, "He must have done this trip," and also, "Why do I deserve hell?" This horror looked like it was going to last forever. Then, I felt tiredness and thought only about loosing myself off; to abandon my body, quitting. But at the same time, I knew, with certainty, that if I did I would stay there forever. From this I took renewed strength and thought about my 5-month old baby and my boyfriend, two people I love so and visualized my son growing up without me. I said, "no. I don't want to stay." I also felt that I had a purpose, a mission that was not yet fulfilled in this life. This was not a work I had to finish, but rather a stage that I had to complete in this life, a form of spiritual growth. At that moment I escaped from the mud pool; that indescribably horrible substance.

7. I drifted up and into a long tunnel. At first, I felt pain and sorrow. I felt, from the perspective of all those affected by me, any hurt I had caused them. It was horrible but I was forced to understand my negative

influence on them. It was incredibly enlightening. I would call it purgatory and I'm glad I didn't have to stay long!

8. It needs to be known to ALL...that on the "other" side...there is no HELL, or "bad" place. If there were, I definitely would have gone there.

9. Jesus was really there. He and I were looking over the edge of the pit, sort of looking at where hell was. It reminded me of when I was little, looking over the edge of a bridge to the water below....it wasn't scary, just looking.

10. All of a sudden she found herself again at the entrance of the tunnel, where it was dark, there was no sound at all. She felt like being one of the many who were there, walking around and around, being doomed to do so eternally. It was the worst thing that a person can ever experience. There was suffering, pain, remorse, guilt. The 'many who were there' were without any body-form like we know, they merely looked like little packets or little dull colored balls and were to her belief rapists and murderers. One of these 'packets' was sort of allowed to leave this place without her knowing exactly how and by whom. She envied this 'entity' for it, the suffering was unbearable.

11. I stepped back down to earth with the utmost reluctance. Earth to me now seemed

like hell because it is where injustice, chaos and everything that seems unfair or arbitrary operates.

12. Then I started to fall down a dark void. When I got to the bottom, the speed at which I was dropping decreased. Soon I was hovering over flames, suspended in the air. I heard the sound of a soul scream out in torment. I was scared beyond belief, knowing that soon I too would be where this person was. I called out for someone to help me. ... I screamed out JESUS SAVE ME. All of a sudden I was pulled out of the dark hole and was put in biblical times.

13. It needs to be known to ALL....that on the "other" side...there is no HELL, or "bad" place. If there were, I definitely would have gone there.

14. I heard moaning that made me get cold chills down my spine. I looked at the stream that was a bit lower than me which was to my left, and there were dead bodies floating in it. I started to freak out and cried. I wiped my eyes and started walking some more and then I asked, "Where am I?" Not even two seconds after I asked myself that there across the "tunnel of death" (that's what I refer to it as) shone a very bright light, but it didn't seem to hurt my eyes. In fact, it felt kind of soothing to look at.

15. I drifted up and into a long tunnel. At first, I felt pain and sorrow. I felt, from the

perspective of all those affected by me, any hurt I had caused them. It was horrible but I was forced to understand my negative influence on them. It was incredibly enlightening. I would call it purgatory and I'm glad I didn't have to stay long!

Summary of Reports of Seven Punishment Places

Seven in the random sample, which projects to three hundred or so in the archives, reported having such an experience.

(I) Stuck in A Mass of Persons

Along the sides of me were other people who were in the darkness that were trying to climb up but couldn't and seemed stuck in a huge mass of themselves.

(II) Stuck in A Mass of Persons

I found myself in a viscous sea of mud. There were a lot of people with me and we were trying to escape from it but could not. I was completely desperate; these people were suffering a lot, they were in torment (while I remember this, my skin goes bristled and my body recalls the horrible sensation). I then thought that this was HELL, and I thought, "Oh My! This looks like Dante's hell. ... . [Is there anything else you would like to add concerning the experience?] I saw what I suppose was hell; where I think people go when they get tied up there by their own will.

(III) Heat and Flames

I was hovering over flames, suspended in the air. I heard the sound of a soul scream out in torment. I was scared beyond belief, knowing that soon I too would be where this person was.

(IV) Heat and Flames

... then it was dark, hot, extremely hot, the surroundings were rocky, dusty, like a canyon under-ground and I was being led downward with the heat intensifying.

(V) Aimless Walking, Suffering, Pain, Remorse, Guilt

... many who were there, walking around and around, being doomed to do so eternally. It was the worst thing that a person can ever experience. There was suffering, pain, remorse, guilt.

(VI) Agony

My world ceased to exist, except for my mind, and an incredible feeling of wrong and unease beyond words. I remained trapped in this condition for an eternity, which seemed like hell for there was no possibility of hope or change, just a timeless eternal agony.

I heard moaning that made me get cold chills down my spine. I looked at the stream that was a bit lower than me which was to my left, and there were dead bodies floating in it. I started to freak out and cried. I wiped my eyes and started walking some more and then I asked, "Where am I?" Not even two seconds after I asked myself that there across the "tunnel of death" (that's what I refer to it as) shone a very bright light, but it didn't seem to hurt my eyes

(VII) Ridicule

Then I could sense that the demons of Hell were standing around me, laughing and enjoying it. They thought it was funny. They were saying stuff like, "All right! We got him! Yeah! Ha! Ha! Way to go!" I was scared shitless. I knew I was about to die and go to Hell.

Voids. Experience of a place of deep dark emptiness, while beginning with feeling fear that was "off the charts," as one visitor put it, most often ended with the light appearing and a not unhappy outcome. Perhaps experience in a void is for some personal-growth purpose.

1. At the end, I made a decision and at that point, the "void" stopped and, with difficulty, I made it back to the shore

2. There are doors sliding in front of me, each door representing a stage of my past life since childhood, and one door representing present day. Somehow I knew I had to enter the right door in the limited time I had, as after that all the doors would close never to open again leaving me all alone in the dark void forever. I also knew that if I entered the wrong door the memories from that stage of my life till today would be erased. I started fearing not death but isolation or never being able to see my two sons & husband again, or even not recognizing them after I wake up. I feel time is slipping out of my hands and I decide

that I'd rather enter the wrong door than stay back in my head.

3. [Was the kind of experience difficult to express in words?] It was hard to believe by others as I saw myself or felt I was walking around outside of the car, but also experienced being highly conscious in a dark void, but I was not afraid. Although it was dark, I felt I could see. There was no up, down or sideways ... no sense of direction. I was alone, Apparently the Buddhists call this Bardo. ... [Did you see a light?] I saw light when I experienced being outside of the car and darkness, pitch black darkness in the void.

4. I was in a dark void or space like in the universe without the stars. In the distance was a light, no definite shape, similar to a puddle of spilled water. The light was pulsating as if alive. I began to move toward the light, was being drawn, all of a sudden it was like I was moving at the speed of light.

5. [Suicide Attempt] Am I going to be here in this place forever! This abyss! What have I done! The fear was off the charts. We are not supposed to take our own life. I was fully aware of what I had done and the thought of being alone in that nothing forever was unbearable but what could I do? It was too late. Suddenly in the void I heard a voice, a male voice, and He said, "It's o.k. It's all right. It's all good." I went from total terror to total

peace and acceptance of my life and responsibility. I was no longer worried about heaven or hell or my death. This voice accepted me, and did not judge me. I in a way had judged myself and clearly had an instant understanding of my life. And how important it is to play our lives out to the end regardless of how hard it is. And to get off of ourselves and to be in the company of each other to help each other. That abyss was total separation from all.

6. I remember being in a dark grey void. A voice said to me: "Richard, why are you here?" I said: "I want to come home." The voice replied: "It's not time yet. You have more work to do. You have a family that loves you and that you need to take care of."

7. Suddenly in the void I heard a voice, a male voice, and He said, "It's o.k. It's all right. It's all good." I went from total terror to total peace and acceptance of my life and responsibility. I was no longer worried about heaven or hell or my death.

8. I was in an atmosphere of absolute white that had no ending anywhere. It was an unending white void. Suddenly, my late parents came to greet me but I do not recall them speaking to me. Other people were there suddenly and I did not recognize any of them. I was at total peace and comfort.

9. I saw a black void endless in depth. I

remember just thinking, "Hmm, okay, big black void?" As I was floating in the void I turned to see what was pulling me forward slowly. I didn't feel any force on me just the sensation of being pulled towards something. I looked forward if you call it forward and saw a light in the void. I would say it was about 400 yards ahead of me and I would be there in about two minutes, at my constant speed. As I drifted towards the white light that twinkled like a star, it didn't hurt to look at it. After the year I finally realized the passage in the Bible, I believe it goes: "As I enter into the valley of the shadow of death I fear no evil." Suddenly and quickly faster than I enter the void, everything went into reverse and I moved away from the white light. Colors that were blocks of color began to focus again and I saw the trees and house clearly again. I was back in my body in the backyard.

List, p. 319.

Dark Tunnels. Experiences in them were not unhappy, and most often led to the light.

1. I felt as if I was squeezed through a dark tube of some kind. I imagine birth could be like it. It felt heavy and hard to squeeze through. When I was out of this dark tube I felt great. ... I begged to stay and then I felt this dark tight tube around me again and at

this moment I heard the nurse call my name.

2. Then all of a sudden I was pulled through this tunnel to a white light.

3. I turned slowly, there was darkness, and a small light at the apparent end. In this tunnel, I could see glimpses of dark blue, purple and gold specks, illuminating the walls of this long, and very quiet tunnel. ... At that time, I turned around, back to the direction I had so calmly came from, and was immediately pulled back through the dark tunnel. It was so fast, that I didn't see any of the magical colors within the dark travel.

4. I became aware that I was traveling rapidly through darkness. It wasn't quite a tunnel, but it did seem to have a form and direction, even though it was dark. ... I got closer to the light, to the point where the darkness disappeared and I was preparing to join the light.

5. Next thing I remember was complete darkness and feeling very confused. Then realized I was in a tunnel and did not know how to get out. I started to feel scared and it was then that I saw a glow of light and a hand reach out to me. [Did you pass into or through a tunnel or enclosure?] The tunnel was the only thing I did not like. It was very dark and you are just walking until you see the light.

6. I travel in a black tunnel...with great

speed... forgotten everything....in this world.

7. Then the blackest black... nothingness...I saw no tunnel, no light. Just blackness. It didn't inspire fear. I felt perfectly fine, and somewhat like a detached observer.

8. I just remember going into a wide and long tunnel, like entering a train tunnel. At the beginning there was still earthly light, then I entered darkness which was not complete even as it was getting denser and denser, and it filled the whole arch, darkness was indeed not black but rather dark grey and thick in its outlines, dense, in the center the void was clear. At the end of this tunnel, I saw this beautiful, extremely attractive light, and to which I came closer very fast.

9. Suddenly I entered a dark tunnel, feeling all the time at peace and in harmony, feeling wonderful ... .

10. I remember a loud roaring in my ears and rushing through a long, dark tunnel at the end of which was a very bright light.

List, p. 331.

Chapter Three

INTO THE LIGHT AND BEYOND

"It felt more real than anything
I've experienced on Earth."

"Grass of the greenest green, with
red roses, as for as the eye can
reach. It was so beautiful. I cried
from happiness."

Apparently a much larger world exists beyond the light. Some of the projected thousand or so who went into and beyond the light reported seeing mountains and valleys, and entire cities instead of the typically small-theater scenes this side of the light.

1. I remember my uncle, my aunt, and my grandma and grandpa were waiting for me when I went through the white light.

2. I remember seeing a brightly colored dome, spires, and living a whole life someplace else. I remember being clothed in simple garb. The feeling of love was enveloping all around me. There was no fear

or sorrow whatsoever. I saw colors that seem to mix together in glimmery iridescence. It was pure joy and happiness. It felt more real than anything I've experienced on earth.

3. There was a bright light and he stopped and told me to go through it. I remember stepping through and it became a bright sunny day. A beautiful place and children playing with lions and everyone was so happy. They all looked at me and told me to go meet them. There were two glowing figures. I could not see their faces, but one was sitting on a throne and one was standing next to the other.

4. The entity then asked me a series of questions. It asked, "Do you like where you are?" I said I thought it was fantastic —I felt better than I ever had before. It then asked, "Do you want to stay here?" My first thought was that this was a silly question given my first answer, but I said, "Yeah, sure! I want to stay." The entity then "reminded" me that I had not fulfilled my purpose yet. Suddenly, I remembered events that had happened before I was conceived. I had chosen to come to this physical existence for a particular reason. I wasn't supposed to know what that reason was until it was time to fulfill my purpose. I also

knew that I could stay in this other place without fulfilling the purpose and it wouldn't be held against me. However, I felt it was better to go back ("to" Earth), fulfill my purpose, and then return.

5. When I was able to open my eyes I saw a very intense blue light. After I saw it far away, I started to pass through a tunnel. At the same time I was walking, I was remembering all the moments I lived with my brother. When I reached again the light I went through it again and I saw my brother (he died 4 years ago). I hugged him and after crying for some minutes he looked at me and told me that I had not to cry for his death. That he died because it was his time and I had to live without laments. That he was fine there and that he was always taking care of me from that place.

6. The light was like a boundary, but it was transparent. I passed through into the light. It is hard for me to find the words to describe the feelings one encounters. ... I felt warm, safe, peaceful, and in the presence of pure unconditional love.

7. Flat lined. Went to a place that was beautifully lit, like the sunshine, but much prettier and more golden (kind of like sepia tones). Seemed like a neighborhood, and I

was shown around to all the people I loved and missed and they were all so happy. I remember being surprised like: "Oh! Hi....wow you're here, how nice," and smiling very broadly. I remember my Dad sitting on a stoop of sorts with his hand outstretched to me. He was many years younger than he was when he died, and I was just a toddler reaching up to him. I know I saw lots of people, but can't remember who they were specifically, except for my Dad.

8. "It's OK we are going home." Next there was a field on the right with people working in it harvesting some kind of grain. Next to the left there were shops and a street that was beautiful and bright. I saw benches like bus stop benches—that was weird.

9. I traveled through space at great speed, once I had lost the fear of going with it. I saw a light and I went into it. It was wondrous light that engulfed everything, there was total knowledge and love. I saw my life from my addiction point of view flash before my eyes, repeated behaviors etc. ... I went back and saw myself in the womb. I was then told to "Remember." I was then flicked thru future decisions and happenings. I was then given a chance to view the universe and given the opportunity to be one with it and have the knowledge of the truth.

10. The white soft light changed into a landscape. Grass of the greenest green, with red roses, as for as the eye can reach. It was so beautiful. I cried from happiness.

11. She said that she could see the city shining in the distance, that the whole place was so beautiful that it hurt your eyes to look at it for very long, and that there was a bright, white light that emanated from the center of the city in the distance.

12. Then I went to the light. Don't know how long I was in the light. The light was instant to me. I opened my eyes. I was scared. Wondering who this person is, where am I? I was in a new body. New place. A new life. I had hard time with all of it. I was starting over.

13. Then soon I'm in another place, walking (floating) with, I think it was, two "beings," for want of a better word. A place of great "light". It is sooo ooooooooooooooooo beautiful. I feel so wonderful. I feel happy. I feel soooo ooooooooooo much love. It is indescribable. There is so much love. The outstanding feature of this entire experience is the feeling (?), knowing (?), no, it's the love itself. A love I've never experienced on this earth. Never in my earthly life have I

experienced the pure love. Not pure love. Maybe it was pure love. Or maybe it was "full" love of which we experience only minute aspects of it on earth. We were in this great light. But, it was different than the light on earth. I didn't feel it like the heat of the sun, and I love the sun. Nor was it like I had to shield my eyes. But, it was a great, magnificent light. We were walking, floating, over a field of wheat. We were "talking." Much talk. Back and forth. I had sooo many questions. I was soooo happy and at peace. I can't say I felt like these beings were old friends, but I had the feeling of love and safety with them. Again, for want of a better description. We talked and talked and talked as we walked. I kept asking questions, and they kept answering my questions, as we kept walking. ... I do know they were telling me about a place we were going to. I could see a (again, for want of a better word) line, or border. Like a horizon, for want of a better word. It was a place of even greater light. We were headed there, and they were excited about it. Then they turned to me and told me I had to go back. We were still in the place of light. I told them I wouldn't go. They tried to convince me to go back. I was adamant. I was staying. Then, another being showed up out of nowhere. I had the feeling he was stronger, or had more authority than the others. Or was different in some way. He talked to me and tried to convince me to return. I still refused, and was steadfast in my decision. I was staying, and they couldn't do anything about it. I was staying. All of a sudden, there was this force pulling me backward. I resisted with all my might, but it was no use. It was stronger than I was. I kept being pulled backward. It was quick. I woke up in my body.

14. I go through the light with her child and I come back through the light.

15. I was in another land. The most wonderful and beautiful place I have ever seen. I remember standing in this street that was cobblestone but it was gold, and I looked down at my feet and just looked at my bare feet on this beautiful gold street. I walked over to one of the buildings and it was so astonishingly beautiful. I remember taking my hand and rubbing the wall and admiring the beauty. I just stood there and rubbed it. As I began walking down the street I met people and we just knew everything. We exchanged smiles and I said I was looking for my sister and daughter. I knew they were there, it was just a matter of finding them. I was not scared. I had a peace and understanding of everything. I had no memory of my life here. I just knew who was there and I kept on looking at this

city that was in front of me. I was walking into the city. It was gold and just cast off all the light in this world. There was no sun or moon but the sky was so beautiful. There was colors of all kinds. The sky was so beautiful. I would stop every now and then and remain to look at my feet walking on this gold street. I then would go to the walls of the buildings and rub them more, so beautiful. There were trees and water so clear. Everyone knew everyone. It was like I had been there forever. I was so happy and had this peace in me that is unexplainable. At that time I knew everything. I was at peace. I remember just standing and looking around at this beautiful city so, so beautiful.

16. Archangel Michael came to me and said "You have another school to go to; don't worry, you will continue on with your college." He escorted me to a magnetic tunnel where Jeshua (Jesus) was waiting for me, who comforted me. I then found myself at the door step of a type of school, where there were a few students learning geometric shapes and physics with the accompanying healing energy involved. I thought the better way would be to directly go to the energy that is involved in the healing, direct from Source. At this point, Mother Mary came in, and motioned for me to follow Her. She asked my thoughts

about what we were learning, I told her it would be best to go right to Source for the healing energy. She said she had something for me to look at, so I followed Her out of the class. I first sat in a healing chair to help my physical body heal on earth. Then we went to a vault that held information from souls' life cycles and growth. I was told I could have access to this information whenever I desired, it was important with the process of uncovering the dense dramas on earth. We also looked into a type of screen that reminded me of a TV screen, and I saw a gathering of people in a field. They were all releasing the density that held back Unconditional Love, then holding the Light within and living within Peace above the dramas. After one man cleared himself out, another individual came up to him who was also cleared, then they shook hands. Both bringing the Reality of Peace into their creative engagement, they both shared Light instead of any fear thoughts or actions. At this point, the Light streamed through them, all the density was then released into the Light. "It's gone! It's all gone!" I exclaimed! "I can see how this works, but who will believe me? I'm a nobody, my dad was a carpenter in Washington and I'll be a small town chiropractor. I think you should get somebody else! Besides that, I'm a bit shy!

17. [Plane Crash] Some were being welcomed with open arms and carefully guided through the transition point and into the wonderful light of the white tunnel; some were being greeted with discussions; and some were being turned back toward the earth plane. When I was met by my own entourage of souls, I could clearly see that they were human, but in this existence were beings of light. They seemed to be the same colour as the electric blue in the first tunnel. I was greeted with a great love and urgency. I was held, and knowledge was imbued into me. I was told, this is not my time, but this was meant to happen.

18. I was standing there puzzled and all when I noticed a tiny light, which seemed to be way off in the distance. I was looking and it slowly seemed to be getting larger, not brighter but larger. In a very short time the light was very large, just a little larger than a person. I could see a person inside the light. The light was bright, but not glaring. It did not dazzle the eyes. It got close enough for me to look at what was inside. There was a very soothing, very strong, but not overbearing thought in my mind that said, "Childing, do not be afraid. We will not harm you in any way." I thought this is very strange. What is a Childing? I was answered almost immediately with the thought, "In a

moment." From now on, I shall refer to them as "they" because that is what they were and are. Anyway, when they said, "What do you have to show us?" Around us sprang up many images. I have to call them "images" here, as we cannot describe what I was experiencing. They were 360° around us. It seemed that every thought, emotion, action, and word that I ever had up to then was embedded in those "images." I could see connections between a thought over here, and way over there—a long time later, a repercussion! I could see words there and right over here. I could see repercussions. Boy, could I see repercussions. Also, I experienced every one of those situations all over again. Now you must understand, this was all going on simultaneously. Here, our brain can only hold one conscious thought at a time, and we seem to feel only one emotion at a time. I saw that many of my thoughts created real hard, tangible, and physical things. Many of the things I had done, thought, emoted, acted, with absolutely no idea of any repercussions, were pointed out as rather drastic errors of judgment. Not bad, just errors. Other things were pointed out to be extremely beneficial to me and to others. Things I thought would get me on the greased slide to the hot spot down below were treated with a rather vast, gentle amusement. It seemed to take forever, and was over in a moment. When it was over, I said, "Who are you? You are not Jesus, because I don't believe Jesus looked like you." They said, "Childing, we are yourselves of your own far future. We are who you are learning to become. Without us, you cannot be. Without you, we are not. We are who Jesus referred to as My Father." Now that is strange, I thought. (You need to understand, there was no air there. I was not "talking" in the sense we talk here. Yet, I could talk.) So I said, "What is this all about? What is happening?" They said, "You are here before your time, an accident. As to what this is all about, you are in a physical body to learn to care about others, and to acquire knowledge. That is the sum totality of physical life." I said, "I saw that many of my thoughts became actual physical things. How is this possible?" They said, "Thoughts ARE things. What you image with emotion is what we must give you in order for you to learn to become us. When you learn to generate a stable image, coupled with firm emotion, we are bound to bring it into being. But remember, there are issues to having this thing." I said, "Such as?" They replied "Such as, do you have the means to support keeping the item now that you have it? Do you actually, truly want it now that you have it? For example, you cannot image intangible things you only feel it? Can you image love, or can you only experience it? You have much to learn Childing. Do you wish to stay or do you wish to return?" Now that place was complete acceptance, complete and total love. I didn't know what else was there, but I had the idea that if I wished to stay all would change completely into something wonderful. And I knew that if I said I wanted to stay, I could. But I sensed that I would have to be born again into a physical body later. My reaction, "But I am only 14 years old." I was standing in the corner of my friend's living room watching the doctor prepare a six-inch hypodermic needle. He stabbed that thing into the body's chest just below the sternum and rammed the plunger home. That body gave a jerk. I was yanked back into that body so fast I bounced right back out again, and then back in. I gave a gasp, and the body started breathing.

19. The plane hits trees and crashes onto a mountainside. ... I couldn't breathe. ... I then find myself in a place that reminds me of Grand Central Station in New York City. It is kind of a gray place, not dark and not light. There's a lot of commotion. People are everywhere. The acoustics were loud. I am watching between two groups of things happening. On my left side, I view people walking two by two in a very calm way. One

is a person who crossed; the other is their guide. I sensed peace and support and they were okay. When I looked to my right, I saw people huddled together in circles. Their heads were all down and I sensed this foreboding feeling, sad and forlorn. I sensed confusion and dread. It wasn't comfortable. I realized that both groups were from the crash. Guides came for the ones on the left and those on the right were having difficulty. I don't know why. I then started moving really fast, past the people on the left with their guides. I questioned, "Why am I moving so fast and they are moving so slow?" I found myself going warp speed through this tunnel place. It was bright and light, but I could see past this a dark blackness. I knew it was infinity out there. As fast as I was moving, suddenly I stopped. I stood on what felt like the edge of a lake shore. It wasn't a bright place; it was dim and I could hear the sound of water, like a lakeshore. It was as if little laps of water were hitting the shoreline, peaceful and rhythmic. I was alone and it was very quiet except for the sound of what seemed like water, a river, or a lake. All of a sudden, I heard giggling and laughing. I looked up and across this lake, river, divide, or whatever and saw these three spheres on my far left. They looked like big cotton balls but ethereal, not dense like cotton. They were so excited to see me. I knew it. I sensed it. Everything said was all telepathic as if energy thoughts coming across. Communication was fast. I didn't have to wait or think about it. I just knew. Their laughter and excitement felt so contagious. I just wanted to go over there. It was so drawing. (For example, when you're sitting in a restaurant and the table near you is having such a good time laughing hysterically, you want to find out what's so funny and laugh too.) I was ready to go over and find out what was so funny. They immediately stopped me and said, "No! We'll come to you." In the next immediate second, they were there on my side. They just came in me, all three. They melded into me and I realized how great communication is without words. Mouthing words is so slow. That is the last thing that happened. The next moment I am in the plane and I hear a voice say, "Oh my God there is someone else in there."

20. From the other side you can travel to any period in time as easily as crossing the street. It is hard to describe the feeling of home that these souls brought with them. I knew them all, but am unsure how as my time there was limited.

21. My angel and I were like flying toward

this really bright light. The light was getting closer and then and in a second it just engulfed us. It was thousands of times brighter than the sun and yet my eyes did not hurt. Somehow I knew I was home.

22. I was suddenly in the light. It swirled around me as clouds. Different shades of white, all swirling fast.

23. When I arrived there I had a scenic view over the scenery that unfolded in front of me. Down below in the bottom of the hill where I stood I could see all kinds of animals and people in white robes playing. There was a river and a pure golden bridge that crossed over it. In the distance I saw a city with towers all in gold and white and amazing bright colors. It seemed that the great city was emitting light that shoots out from it with such energy you could feel the power. I wanted to go there but the only way down was flying and I did not feel comfortable with that. I saw a stream of water that ran along the edge of the garden. When I came close, the water was crystal clear. I have never seen such amazing water before. My guardian angel explained that it was living water. I went to another place which was kind of a neutral place similar to this plane. I knew I was supposed to take a "class" or learn something.

24. I saw that the root of all life in the universe was energy, that all energy was related and equal. There is no energy in the universe that would want or need worship, and the possibilities of energy are unlimited.

25. Physical movement had no meaning. On the other hand, I knew that this new place had some type of dimension. I just didn't know what it was. It seemed like I was in an area of "lesser concentration" surrounded an area of "greater concentration" located at a "distance." The "area of greater concentration" felt like it might be a "city" of some kind. I sensed that there were many entities there. I also had a feeling that I would also eventually go there as well.

26. We traveled along a small road for a while. Right there in front of me stood the entrance to heaven. Before we entered my guardian angel suddenly stopped me and said after my visit here I will have no doubt that heaven exists. So we entered thru the gates into a landscape that seemed like a massive garden of some sort. The grass was so bright, glowing with energy. I noticed we were not walking but floating above the ground. Your movement is controlled with your thoughts. I could not think of any bad thoughts as we could on earth. ... My

guardian angel was dressed in a pure white robe and seemed kind of transparent. ... There were countless people there, all dressed in white robes; some were walking in the garden. Others were flying through the air at incredible speed. All around was just happiness in its purest form. ... My guardian angel asked me if I wanted to explore more of heaven. Instantly I said yes. I looked up and could see no sun only a blue sky with clouds. I traveled unbelievably fast. I saw a sudden drop or a steep slope at one location in the garden. When I arrived there I had a scenic view over the scenery that unfolded in front of me. Down below in the bottom of the hill where I stood I could see all kinds of animals and people in white robes playing. There was a river and a pure golden bridge that crossed over it. ... I saw a stream of water that ran along the edge of the garden. When I came close, the water was crystal clear. I have never seen such amazing water before. My guardian angel explained that it was living water. Shortly after that my guardian angel said I should return to earth because it was not my time yet. All of a sudden I traveled back to earth at such a speed, through the tunnel, and back into my body.

Chapter Four

BACK HOME AGAIN

"I felt like I was 'home'. This was where I had come from, this was where I belonged."

"In these rooms the spirits, or people, were planning their next life or reincarnation."

"Death is not the end, only a transition to our true home."

Home. More than 1,600 visitors said that the afterlife is where we come from. More than 1,300 used the word "home" when telling of their experience there. Apparently we exist in the afterlife before we enter physical life, and after physical life we leave our bodies behind and go back home. This requires a paradigm shift, a fundamental change in our understanding of our very existence.

1. I would go through many terrible experiences to the point of wanting to commit suicide, but if I committed suicide I would not be allowed to come home.

2. If I would get through this mission I would be allowed to return home.

3. I saw people on this seashore, and I seemed to know these people even though I have never seen them in this dimension. I felt such love and I felt so much love from them.

4. I was just in another place, somewhere I'd always been. [Did you meet or see any other beings?] I knew them, but none of them were people from my life here. They were just people. It was just life, only better.

5. I can't really describe the joy or calm I felt. I wanted to go so badly. It felt like home.

6. I felt a very powerful all loving, , sensation that I was Home!

7. Since then I feel sort of Homesick and a sense of not belonging to this world. For I know this is not my home.

8. There was no sadness, no pain, no regret and no fear. All earthly thoughts were gone. I was going home.

9. I didn't want to come back. That was my focus. I was Home. I liked being Home. Just let me be Home.

10. Two people I never saw before were beaming at me and said they were aunt and uncle. I did not know them.

List, p. 235.

The Afterlife is Filled with Love. It is as if it is the air that is breathed there, the gravity of the afterlife.

1. I came into the light. The light was so brilliant but neither warm nor cold. It was almost as if it consumed me. A feeling of Love so powerful and consuming washed over me.

2. I saw people on this Seashore and I seem to know these people even though I have never seen them in this dimension. I felt such love and I felt so much love from them.

3. I was in this amazing golden light, ... the warm light was "God" or my idea of God. I felt loved and cared for and precious, which was fabulous, and it seemed like everything made sense. "Ahhah" moment. ....this presence didn't tell me it was god - that was my later determination -

4. I just enjoyed the most wonderful peace and unconditional love. I think unconditional love doesn't do it justice, but I can't think of better words unless maybe "Awe Inspiring." ... I was like a baby wrapped in love. But the love was so intense, I did wonder a little about it I think. It felt new. Like a rebirth.

5. The feeling of love was enveloping all around me.

6. I felt the most immense sense of love and

understanding. (Until this day this feeling has never left me.)

7. I then saw a bright gentle light coming down on me from the ceiling and it filled me with happiness and love that I never felt on earth. I completely became addicted to it, it was so powerful. I let myself involved in it like I was bathing in pure euphoria. I never thought and cared anymore about my worries or fears about the errors I made in my entire lifetime.

8. [Did you see a light?] It was blinding, but out of it radiated the most wondrous feelings of love.

9. I heard a booming voice say, "I love you but you haven't experienced my gift to you yet. If you were to go now you would never get to see what it is like to..." and I woke up.

List, p. 161.

Indescribable Peace. Many used the word "indescribable." None mentioned being asleep, or seeing anyone asleep.

1. I started to feel a peace and well-being which is indescribable.

2. My "pleasure" intensified to the highest degree the further I drew away from life.

3. I felt a peace and tranquility that I've never felt since.

4. I wasn't scared at that point. I was actually completely at peace.

5. It was the most wonderful experience. I was filled with so much happiness.

6. All around me I could see and feel a beautiful peace and tranquility with love and peace. I had no care in the world.

7. It felt like joy all around me. I felt fabulous, no pain, no worries, complete ment.

8. It was like having happiness running through your veins. [What emotions did you feel during the experience?] Happiness. Love. Joy. Every positive emotion you could drag out.

List p. 189.

Floating One Means of Movement

1. I was floating, without a body, but still I could move around.

2. I was inured playing basketball. This is where my experience began. I was looking down on the whole schoolyard from above, as though floating in the air, and could see my fellow-players weeping and crying out.

3. I blacked out ... . At this time I looked down on myself lying there with my friends around me. I could hear what they were saying and what was going on. I heard the TV and the commercials and show I was watching. I felt myself kinda floating above them near the ceiling.

4. Then I opened my eyes and I was no <u>longer</u> in the operating room. I seemed to be floating.

5. While being operated on I remember floating in the corner of the room above the operating table looking down at myself wondering what was going on.

6. Drowning. For a while, I ceased to exist... then darkness, a clear sensation of floating, during which my mind continued to function. I said to myself: "Ah, well, here you are then, this is death for you! It's not so bad as all that, after all.

L. [Did your vision differ in any way from your normal, everyday vision (in any aspect...)?] I could float in the air, and watch my body.

List, p. 301.

"You were the music." More than six hundred reported hearing music.

1. I feel me riding as a little boy on a beautiful merry go round, lovely organ music, beautiful white clothes

2. And I asked myself why, since there was so much more for me to do, when the most beautiful music surrounded me and I resigned myself to staying

3. It was like a loud roar, but very loving the way it was said, and the music was like nothing I ever heard to this day. It went right

through you, and you were the music as well.

4. Suddenly I found myself in a boat, floating down a river in a jungle. In the background I could hear the most magnificent music I had ever heard. It was a jungle drum beat of incredible dimensions. I became very elated with its incessant melodic sounding rhythm.

5. I saw a caterpillar, with a very charming face saying, "Play my music to regain your health," smiled, and I neared my body.

6. It was wonderful. I started hearing music. Beautiful music and, I started seeing a mirage of colors.

7. I moved through the tunnel, and there was wonderful music all around - similar to Enya, Clannad, that sort of sound. But even more beautiful. I moved through the tunnel, and there was wonderful music all around - similar to Enya, Clannad, that sort of sound. But even more beautiful.

8. There was also music like bells.

9. There was very soft, beautiful music with lots of violins. I have the song in my head, but I have never heard it before or since.

10. I could see the water and a bright glow surrounding it. The burbling of the water had a musical sound. The stream of water fairly sang.

11. Everything was so peaceful with faint music.

12. All around me were beings of pulsing,

colored light, and indescribable music/singing full of joy and praise. ... There was nothing but light, music, praise for God and All That Is, and many beings/points of consciousness. The beings were creating the music and were made of the music. I was made of music, light and joy.

13. Then she saw IT, the music and colors that were indescribably beautiful and a light with such an intense beauty and mildness as never before.

14. I was becoming very frightened because I could not understand, and then suddenly, there was singing all around me, voices, many, many, voices singing praises to God— the most beautiful music I'd ever heard! And then I joined in their song as if I knew that song always, and I really had never heard it before!

15. I was suddenly in a tunnel roteerde (type cloud) and inside were millions of lights. I looked around astonished and did not understand what happened. I heard beautiful music that seemed like classical music. [Google translation]

Colors: White Clothing. Let's remind ourselves that there is no physical clothing in the afterlife. The 800+ visitors were seeing persons who were choosing to appear to be in white clothing.

1. [Did your dad meet or see any other beings?] A holy man with long brilliant white robe on and long hair could not make out the face.

2. He was of medium build with white shoulder length hair, with a white shiny white beard like angel hair and had on a white robe with sash.

3. A man who had a kind gentle face dressed in a white cloth was before me.

4. During this time, I feel me riding as a little boy on a beautiful merry go round, lovely organ music, beautiful white clothes. I was happy, smiling and laughing with all the other kids. We experienced total bliss. My other little friends were also decked out in white clothing going around and around.

5. I looked down at my gown and it was a white sack dress and my hair was hanging.

6. He wore a white tunic and I walked on his left.

7. I was standing in a white robe.

8. A beautiful woman with long black hair in a white robe trimmed in gold came down through the Light.

9. I saw a black table and seven people all dressed in white clothing standing on the other side of the table.

10. A radiant being in long white robes was there to greet me.

11. His white, ruffled shirt shone like the sunlight.

12. There appeared before me a lovely woman dressed in white (an angel).

13. A blond woman, wearing white was on the other side.

14. Someone in all white escorted me to this place.

15. I saw an image of myself in a white robe as if it were hanging on a coat hook

16. My guardian angel was dressed in a pure white robe and seemed kind of transparent.

17. These people were in white robes.

19. They were all wearing white. (If they were robes or jumpsuits they were wearing, I couldn't tell.)

19. He wore a simple white robe.

Colors: Many Others Spoke of White. It appeared in a number of ways, most often as a white light. 1,300 in this category.

1. I could see a kind of white light shining, without knowing whether it was sunlight or just a light. But it shone through and lit up all my surroundings. ... I saw a whiter light, which seemed infinite, through a long and completely white tunnel.

2. He showed me what looked like a huge white obelisk floating in the blackness.

3. I was pulled through this tunnel to a white light. ... To my right was a wall of a beautiful blue that matched the sky.

4. I remember my uncle, my aunt, and my grandma and grandpa were waiting for me when I went through the white light.

5. The light was so bright it was almost white.

6. He was of medium build with white shoulder length hair, with a white shiny white beard like angel hair and had on a white robe with sash.

7. Suddenly, I saw this beautiful white light slowly coming towards me. A man who had a kind gentle face dressed in a white cloth was before me.

8. We got to a white bridge and I was ready to go over when the presence said it was okay to go over but told me I had three small children on this side. So I remained on this side.

9. These people were in white robes. I found myself between the darkness and the most luxuriant white light you can imagine. It was made of all the colours of the rainbow and more but it was not hard on the eye.

10. We had calla lilies and white roses everywhere.

11. I entered a tunnel. At the end of the tunnel was a bright warm white vibrating light it was beautiful and it gave me a very calm and reassuring feeling.

12. Then everything went white, not exactly white, but colorless.

13. I was in an atmosphere of absolute white

that had no ending anywhere. It was an unending white void.

14. I remember standing (or whatever) in a bright white sort of fog.

15. Everything was brilliantly illuminated with a white light.

16. Everything was a neon white.

17. That's when I encountered two "beings of Light". There was no form to them, just ovals radiating a soft peaceful white light.

18. She was like a huge orb of white light with many hands going in and out of her. She was like billons of conscious minds put together. I was also part of her because I saw white light in a form of an umbilical cord attaching her to me.

19. I stood before a light, white landscape.

20. I would look down and see a white stone path with people waving.

21. I then remember going into what I can only describe as a white enclosed slide type of tunnel, the diameter being about five feet.

22. I saw a tunnel and began spinning in the tunnel. It was white all around me.

23. I was in a very bright, white light place.

24. I saw what looked like a bright, white circle. It looked very happy.

25. Everything in this garden had an overall whiteness and brightness about it.

26. I was on a pure white bed with pure white sheets in a large white room that had curvature where the walls met the ceiling.

There was a thin black line where the walls met the ceiling, but the ceiling wasn't perceptible only the curvature, brilliant white and pure white floor.

27. He told me he was in an in between place, "the other side," and people were around him in white gowns, like sitting on a train.

28. I was suddenly in the light. It swirled around me as clouds. Different shades of white, all swirling fast.

29. When the door opened, there was a tremendous snow-white flood over us. The sudden white light was blinding; I had to turn away from it.

30. I was unable to go beyond the layer of white that surrounded me, white was everywhere.

Colors: Blue-White. While many colors were mentioned, the colors white, blue and a blue-white combination outnumbered all the other colors combined. Let's start with the combination.

1. There was this beautiful blue-white light coming from the sky.

2. My soul then almost instantly was engulfed in the most beautiful bluish-white light.

3. It was so bright white it had almost a blue hue to it.

4. There was a big white house that sat under a brilliantly blue sky and there was a nice flower garden and white sheets blowing in the breeze on laundry lines.

5. I was still diving faster and faster and deeper and deeper toward a bluish white light that was attracting me.

6. We went through a powder blue-white light.

7. Then I found myself in a blue tunnel. The colour was an electric blue, similar to the kind you get on certain L.E.D. Christmas lights now. It was a very vivid and wonderful colour. ... At this point, the blue tunnel turned into the white tunnel, a very clear line of transition. ... The blue tunnel could accommodate two-way traffic, whereas the white tunnel was one way for souls leaving the earth plane. Once you crossed over into the white tunnel there was no going back. The light from this tunnel was so bright that under normal circumstances it would have been blinding, but here it was warm, safe and full of love. As I got closer to the transition point between the blue and white tunnels, the activity became clearer. I could clearly see many, many souls on both sides of the transition point. There were quite a few souls, like myself, coming from the earth plane. All of these souls were being met by groups of souls who had come from the white tunnel. It was like each soul had its

own entourage of souls from the other side to meet them ... When I was met by m own entourage of souls, I could clearly see that they were human, but in this existence were beings of light. They seemed to be the same colour as the electric blue in the first tunnel. I was greeted with a great love and urgency. I was held, and knowledge was imbued into me. I was told, this is not my time, but this was meant to happen.

8. Then I wondered what was this bluish-white sesame seed in front of me. Up until that point every time I wondered anything the voice told me. Yet this time as I looked at the blue sesame seed, there was no voice.

9. I didn't have a body, but seemed to exist as a light bluish energy.

10. I was bathed in a bluish, white light that had the sensation of acceleration and direction.

11. The light was blue-white in color. It seemed to fluoresce rather than radiate, except from the bottom.

12. There were big, puffy, white clouds surrounding me, and I caught glimpses of blue sky.

Colors: Blue. One visitor said: "I later realized the blue aura was me."

1. I was surrounded with blue color and my body was transparent.

2. All of a sudden I was in the most beautiful place. The sky was so blue.

3. When I was able to open my eyes I saw a very intense blue light.

4. I felt that I was wearing a long pale blue robe/dress, so long it covered my feet.

5. I noticed there was a soft blue aura all round me (I later realized the blue aura was me).

6. I was also aware of other beings there that were not alive in the physical senses of the word. They had a bluish tinge to them.

7. It was light blue all around me.

8. There was also a blue light around my hands.

9. It was such a beautiful color blue surrounding

10. I had a body of what seemed to be made out of a shapeless energy and a bright indigo-bluish light.

11. I see this bluish, gray light/energy come out of my dad's body. I see my body and I see a bluish, gray light go into my body.

12. Bha was talking animatedly with a blue light being; he was tall and the shape of a man, but he had no features. A neon turquoise blue light outlined his shape and he had lights moving on the inside of his shape like sunlight playing on water.

13. I didn't have a body, but seemed to exist as a light bluish energy.

14. I had been examining my hands and

arms, which were a translucent light blue. I still looked normal, but without actual body mass.

15. When I was met by my own entourage of souls, I could clearly see that they were human, but in this existence were beings of light. They seemed to be the same colour as the electric blue in the first tunnel.

Colors: Miscellaneous. List, p. 329.

Time. Both duration and past-future sequence terms were well represented. There are so many reports with references to time and space we have included only a few.

1. ... when I looked at the ground I could see thousands of fallen leaves. ... [At what time during the experience were you at your highest level of consciousness and alertness?] I was conscious of "being me" throughout.

2. The terror I felt before everything went black was gone.

3. I exited the flight of stairs and as soon as I did, I heard moaning that made me get cold chills down my spine. ... But I heard someone say, "You're not supposed to be here yet. Come with me and go back to your home, it's not your time." ... Soon I was in complete darkness and felt as if I were falling up and ... I heard a booming

voice say, "I love you but you haven't experienced my gift to you yet. If you were to go now you would never get to see what it is like to..." and I woke up.

4. All things that happened next seemed to happen all at once, or in very fast succession. ... I was told that in time I would visit again and to be vigilant in my life.

5. I felt as if I was thinking faster or that during the experience?] At first, confusion, then a great calm, with much peace and well being.

6. From the other side you can travel to any period in time as easily as crossing the street.

7. My life did "flash" before me; however this "review" did not stop at my birth. My recollection was going back in time and "space" well before my birth. A time and place best described as Eden-like.

8. What happened next was probably the most confusing and unbelievable experience yet. I was standing IN THE WATER, I had a solid footing under me, and I was looking down the beach to my left. ... There were absolutely no people on the beach, which was odd, since before, the beach was packed with people. ... There was actually no break in my stream of consciousness between reviewing my life before this new landscape, and while I was observing it.

9. She said to me, "This is what it will be like

when you come here." ... Then this Being next to me said that it was time to go now and I will see them again but it was not my time yet.

10. [Did you have any sense of altered space or time?] I was definitely in two places at the same time.

11. [Did you have any sense of altered space or time?] No question about it. What we call time here is not accurate. It works for our world but it does not have the depth (for lack of a better word) for the other. I don't think time really exists there, at least not in the way that we know it here.

12. Finally Jesus told me that if I was going back I had to go now or I would be too damaged.

13. At this point an unknown, but very clear voice, said to me: "No, you're not going to die, it's really not your time yet (with the implication 'you'll live to be very old') and you're going to get out of this."

14. [Did you have any sense of altered space or time?] No question about it. What we call time here is not accurate. It works for our world but it does not have the depth (for lack of a better word) for the other. I don't think time really exists there, at least not in the way that we know it here.

Space. Most visitors used terms for direction and distance. There are so many reports with references to time and space we have included only a few.

1. I started to move forward ... I turned around to look and behind me ... I knew I couldn't turn back so I turned back around. In front of me ...

2. I was slowly aware of a light ahead of me. I seemed to be pulled along toward it. ... A group of people came toward me with warm greetings.

3. I felt very confused and somehow moved to the side of my bed and I realized I was completely outside of my body. I just stared at it trying to come to terms that I was looking upon myself. I knew that the body in the bed was me, but I did not look on it with the same sense of self as I was accustomed to when looking in a mirror.

4. I was looking down on the whole schoolyard from above, as though floating in the air ... From my position (above and to the right of the whole scene) I could see everything that happened over the whole schoolyard with great clarity ... there was light, much light, all around me ... Towards the end of the walkway, one saw an enormous central light.

5. I opened my back door to get air and when I looked outside there was this beautiful blue-white light coming from the sky. I could see very far as if a nuclear

bomb had went off outside. It was 3:30am and I could see for miles it seemed.

6. "There is no way that I can climb that hill," before she was floating above it to wherever her destination lay. ... as she reached the crest of the hill ... She continued on, over the roses, and at the top of the hill ... the whole place was so beautiful ... there was a bright, white light that emanated from the center of the city in the distance.

7. I also remember wandering around in a charcoal-colored fog. ... I was in a place where it was all bright white.

8. Suddenly I found myself in a boat, floating down a river in a jungle ... Then I came upon the distant shore. ... I do not remember stepping onto the shore. However the most incredible feeling of love surrounded me. It emanated from the being.

9. I was drawn upward into a sort of tunnel ... A spot of light appeared in the distance ... there was someone or something beside me

10. He was about six feet in front of me, standing there. ... He seemed to be about the size of a regular man, being he was only about six feet away. Height and everything seemed normal, but in another sense He seemed huge. ... I kept wanting to look way up, straight up at Him instead of straight ahead. ... He was standing beside me on a mountain top, and we were looking down on a valley. ... On the other side of the

valley was another mountain ... I could see clearly every detail of both sides of the valley ... I have a faint memory of an object in the middle of the valley, and of the people going to and from this object ... The object seemed to be about the size of a standard sized car with a similar shape.

Experience REAL. NOT A Dream. Most were quite sure about this.

1. " ... it was like a dream but I still remember it as being too real to be a dream.
2. "It was without a doubt that I passed on to another dimension. a real life which awaits us after this one.
3. [Was the experience dream like in any way?] Yes, but it was too real to put off as a dream or alarm-state. I saw it all so real, and the voice was not in my head, but out loud.
4 [How do you currently view the reality of your experience?] Experience was definitely real
5. Experience was definitely real. I didn't give it much thought as to whether it was real or not. I knew it was real.
6. At my left side was a wolf. It was snarling and growling and foaming at the mouth like a rabid animal. I could feel its breath and spittle flying into my face. I knew this wolf was going to tear me limb from limb. I remember screaming for my father to help me over and

over. This experience is as real today as the day it happened even after all these years.

6. I told myself that I was "dreaming" but, as if arguing with myself, saying, "No, this is entirely too real to be a dream." Also while the experience was unfolding all the details were vividly clear.

7. It could be argued that it was only a dream, I can accept that. But I have to say that it was the most vivid dream I have ever had, and it haunts me to this very day. It felt real and true.

8. Dieing is being born into the real life. ... I want everyone to know that it is real there, more real than here, and what I said about dieing and their message.

9. It felt more real than anything I've experienced on earth.

10. [Was the experience dream like in any way?] No. It was not the same at all. In dreams you awake at some point and know that it was a dream.

11. You can recall what felt real in a dream and experience a dream believing that it was real, but I have never "known" and "experienced" anything as real as the out of body experience. It was clearer than conscious life and much more profound.

12. [How do you currently view the reality of your experience?] Experience was definitely real Prior to my NDE I was an atheist and didn't believe in any afterlife, but after the NDE I had to reconsider everything I believed.

Chapter Five

THE HIGHER SELF

"The individual is a composite,—a
multiple individuality."—Dr. Boris
Sidis, 1904.

"Your movement is controlled with
your thoughts."

"I could now stay with these beings, or I
could take on another assignment and return
to the earth plane."

As soon as we leave our bodies we begin to
regain the far greater powers of the higher self
which were stifled in physical life. But the higher
self is our normal self and is perceived as higher
from here in our lower selves.

Our Minds Are Set Free. Here is a remarkable sentence: *Thinking not only continues after there is no brain involved, it becomes more powerful.*

Of course all the visitors continued thinking after they left their bodies, but more than three thousand took note of it.

[*This finding, along with the upcoming mind-to-mind communication data, confronts the long-standing philosophical argument that everything can be explained by brain and that there is no such thing as mind. The great American psychologist William James had worried that "no mortal may ever know" the answer.*]

1. I felt as though I had been liberated from my body, and being outside my body freed me from the limitations imposed by a physical existence. My mind felt cleared and my thoughts seemed quick and decisive.

2. I remember thinking, "I wonder if I've died?"

3. I remember thinking. It was more like knowing instead of thinking.

4. I kept thinking at every turn that this was wonderful and amazing.

5. I'm still wondering, "What is happening to me?"

6. I also understood that my body is like a car my consciousness drives.

7. When I was "in" my body, I didn't know what was going on. When I was "hovering" I

had vivid thoughts.

8. I felt that my body was separate from my spirit and they were on two different planes of existence.

9. I remember just thinking: "No. Where am I? Where are we going?

10. I remember thinking, "That was cool being Thomas," like it was some fun excursion, this human life.

11. I noticed we were not walking but floating above the ground. Your movement is controlled with your thoughts.

List, p. 137.

Mind-to-Mind Communication. Without a body we have no brain; but apparently a stand-alone mind, when not connected to a brain, can communicate directly with other stand-alone minds.

1. They spoke to me with thought and I knew they were like me.

2. When the person reached me we spoke through thought.

3. Communication was telepathic, I didn't hear them speak, but it was as if I knew what they were telling me.

4. They spoke to me, yet they had no mouths to speak, I just knew what they were saying.

5. A telepathic dialogue took place in which certain questions were asked and I was compelled to answer truthfully.

6. My guide spoke to me through my mind.

7. I didn't know all of them, they were greeting me telepathically.

8. The "being" spoke to me although the words were not heard with my ears. It was as if someone was speaking in my head, although it was not my voice I heard.

9. Strangely though it seemed like I didn't need to hear words. I could just feel what they were saying.

List, p. 211.

Regained Vast Knowledge. Twenty-seven hundred reported they learned such things as the purpose of life and answers to profound questions. None was able access the vast knowledge once back in physical life.

1. It seemed like finally everything made sense. It was like an "Ah hah!" moment.

2. I had an enormous sense of understanding the meaning of life.

3. I remember knowing the purpose of life and why we are all here, as if someone was speaking to me.

4. So much "information." Personal, universal. Mostly about Thought and Love.

5. I felt enveloped in some kind of "knowing" that surpassed the human senses.

6. Moment by moment you discover how quickly you are gaining knowledge; and how easy it is to accept.

7. I watched and listened suspended above my own body. At the same time it was as though all questions of the universe had been answered in that one moment.

8. At that moment everything appeared to be self-evident.

List, p. 209.

Here is something Socrates said just before his return to the afterlife 24 centuries ago.

"But if the knowledge which we acquired before birth was lost by us at birth, and afterwards by the use of the senses we recovered that which we previously knew, will not that which we call learning be a process of recovering our knowledge, and may not this be rightly termed recollection by us?"*—Phaedo*

Past and Future Lives and Events Seen. "The individual is a composite,—a multiple individuality."—Dr. Boris Sidis, 1904. Some 700 spoke of reincarnation. Here is the complete list of the reincarnation excerpts in the random sample, some of which are rather mysterious.

1. I remember seeing a brightly colored dome, spires, and living a whole life someplace else. I remember being clothed in simple garb. In the screen, were the most surprising images. They have never left me.

They were of a previous life. From backward images I saw myself as a young blond-haired young man. I was killed in a car accident and I saw myself leaving the scene with a briefcase walking towards the screen. Before that I saw that I had lived in a suburb in a pale yellow ranch home with a long driveway. Outside the driveway next to the car, I was saying good bye to my wife, my almost-two-year-old daughter, and son about 4 years old. After the kisses and goodbyes I got in my car with my briefcase to go to work.

2. There were small groups of people or spirits (?) in individual rooms called "pods." In these rooms the spirits, or people, were planning their next life or reincarnation. ... [Did you experience a review of past events in your life?] I did not experience a review, although I was shown volumes of books containing my lives.

3. I am sucked up into a tunnel and I get the sudden knowledge that I am in a birth canal heading toward a light. It is very quick, and when I get to the light I see a woman in an ambulance. I am thinking that I am to be reincarnated as her child. I have never believed in reincarnation. She is African American and I am white. (I know that I am white and I am thinking, "How can this be? How can I become her child now?") The race difference doesn't matter to me. I am

thinking she is a nice person, I would like to be her child. But then I have a baby in my arms. I know that it is her child and at first I am thinking that I am bringing her baby to her. I know that I am taking her baby to Heaven. I go through the light with her child and I come back through the light. And now I am walking down the tunnel again. I have a little girl of about five years of age holding my right hand and walking with me. I pass two women and it is the first time someone notices me. They smile. I pass a man who looks at me and says angrily, "Why does she get to go?" I ignore him. I don't know who he is referring to, the little girl or me, and I don't care. I go through the birth canal feeling again (it is painful both times) towards a bright light. I go through with the little girl when I come back through she isn't with me. I am scared because I don't know where she is, then I realize she is with Jesus. I feel good that she is with Jesus, but I feel sorrow for her mother. Then I walked back passed the three people and I myself. I am walking towards a light there is a woman with long dark hair in the light I am thinking that she is my grandmother only she isn't old anymore. She looks at me and tells me "It's not your time, it just isn't your time". She is smiling. Then I am seeing a woman (she is beautiful with long brown hair) at the end of my hospital bed, and I can see myself lying in the bed, I am confused, I look at her and I am speaking to her and I don't know how because I can see myself in the hospital bed with tubes down my throat, hooked to machines. I am trying to convey to her the dream I had but she already knows and asks me while smiling, "Did you see the light?" I answer "Yes." I look at myself in the hospital bed, then look back towards her and she is gone. Then I wake up.

4. I have feelings and am scared about my past life. My mind has stored the things I liked and what scared me or killed me in past life. And they haunt me every day. It's just what I know. Take it as you wish.

5. A true enrichment is what I learned about former lives and the friends over there I can discuss essential life questions with. Of practical use is the service to anyone. I can ask questions for them and pass on the answers like a medium.

6. Hard to explain, remember dieing but, not a near death. It was death and knowing I was dead. It was dark and I saw the light. I was wondering why I died. What happened? And, thinking it must have been a fast death, then a fear that if I didn't go into the light I would be lost. And that I remember someone or a feeling to go to the light or something bad might happen. Then I went to the light. Don't know how long I was in the light. The light was instant to me. I opened

my eyes. I was lying on someone's lap. I was lost and scared. Wondering who this person is, where am I? I was in a new body. New place. A new life. I had hard time with all of it. I was starting over. There is a big curiosity about life after death/near death/I had death and life and every thing in between. The mind is not the person. It's *the electricity that makes the body work? I have feelings and scared about my past* life. My mind has stored the things I liked and what scared me or killed me in past life. And they haunt me every day. It's just what I know. Take it as you wish.

7. I heard farther away someone saying there is a body available, but you must act quick. I said I'll go, but one of the others close to me said, "No, it's too soon for you." I said, "I don't care, I want to go." And they said you must go now or it will be too late. Next thing I remember is being in a crib. And this person was looking at me and talking and smiling. Later I could remember being somewhere inside a wrapping of sorts I would reach to touch it but I couldn't seem to reach it. It was comfortable. But then I would be scared, like claustrophobic. ... Since then many things have happened. I remember three past lives, and since 2003 I've been getting visions etc.

8. After closing my eyes, the next recollection was myself being in the

presence of, in the arena of, enveloped in, PURE UNCONDITIONAL LOVE. Re-reading this, it sounds so lame. How can I explain? For all these years I just have not been able to describe this to fully honour its incredibleness, its ISNESS. A communication occurred, through instantaneous osmosis, rather than our human verbalization. The communication concerned my prenatal chosen human life's work as well as some basic universal laws, which I had overlooked in my human form.

9. I remember a black tunnel and being totally out. Then I was in another world. I remember using my thoughts to create planets. I sent them out with my thoughts and felt as if lighting struck me, but in a beautiful way. I saw my planets being created. I was going wee and haa like when you first see fireworks. A female voice told me that what I create is mine. I then looked at the direction where this voice was coming from and I saw her. She was consciousness itself. She was like a huge orb of white light with many hands going in and out of her. She was like billons of conscious minds put together. I was also part of her because I saw white light in a form of an umbilical cord attaching her to me. Then I was being treated as a baby because she was massaging my neck. The love I felt for her was greater than that of any love I have felt

in this world. I felt something inside of me, like I did not accomplish a task. I did not remember what it was, but I knew that I had to do it. I remember saying that I have to go back. Suddenly, I turned around and I came face to face with this light being who looked human. As I looked around there were millions of light humanoid creatures all over the place. This place had no planets or stars; there was darkness and the only light source was the light humanoid beings. When I first saw him I felt as though I knew him. I hugged him; the love I had for him was very strong. He felt closer to me than my own family. We started to communicate telepathically. I was telling him that I needed to go back and he replied that it wasn't possible. I saw in his facial expression that he did not want me to go. I told him again that I wanted to go back. He then showed me an image of a young handsome and wealthy couple that just had a baby boy and he told me that I could be born as that baby. The offer was very tempting, but I refused. I told him that I needed to go back to this life. He said if I go back in this time, life would not be the same and very difficult. I listened to his advice, but I willed myself back into this lifetime. While I was willing myself to come back into this lifetime, I remember the female entity told me to bring her children back to her. I then realized that this entity is the one source, the true God. As I left that heavenly realm and came back to Earth, I remember flying in the air and into my body. While in the air looking below at the area of the crash site, I was floating down into my body.

10. Then we went to a vault that held information from souls' life cycles and growth. I was told I could have access to this information whenever I desired.

11. I then saw a glimpse of my brother and me and somehow seemed to understand it was a previous life, where I was much older than him and was like a mother to him (in this life, he is older than me). I saw in that life I was very protective towards him. I suddenly became aware he was on the plane to come and see me, and felt, "I can't do this to him—can't let him come and see me dead". Then I also saw how my husband's purpose was linked to mine, and how we had decided to come and experience this life together. If I went, he would probably follow soon after. I was made to understand that, as tests had been taken for my organ functions (and the results were not out yet), that if I chose life, the results would show that my organs were functioning normally. If I chose death, the results would show organ failure as the cause of death, due to cancer. I was able to change the outcome of the tests by my choice!

12. Suddenly, I remembered events that had happened before I was conceived. I had chosen to come to this physical existence for a particular reason. I wasn't supposed to know what that reason was until it was time to fulfill my purpose. I also knew that I could stay in this other place without fulfilling the purpose and it wouldn't be held against me. However, I felt it was better to go back ("to" Earth), fulfill my purpose, and then return.

13. My life did "flash" before me; however this "review" did not stop at my birth. My recollection was going back in time and "space" well before my birth.

14. Just as my life had passed before my eyes when I was being drowned, I was now being shown my future life, with as much info as I could remember.

15. Childing, we are yourselves of your own far future. We are who you are learning to become. Without us, you cannot be. Without you, we are not.

16. Two people I never saw before were beaming at me and said they were aunt and uncle. I did not know them. I had hard time with all of it. I was starting over.

17. I didn't have a body, I was immaterial. I had only my thought and stop, nothing all. I forgot my body. The time moved fast and I thought very fast. I saw me at two years old, then at four in the sea, etc. Suddenly my life it's over and then I saw three slides of my

probable future.

Extreme Vision. Even though they no longer had physical eyes they could (1) see from more than one point of view at the same time; (2) see with a 360° sphere of vision; (3) just by wanting a closer look could zoom in at will; (4) see clearly in the dark; and (5) everything they saw had a crystal clarity and vividness far greater than is possible with physical eyesight. It's as if our eyes are, as one visitor put it, a pair of foggy goggles.

1. [Did your vision differ in any way from your normal, everyday vision?] It was as if I could see everything. There were no limits to what I could see if I chose to.

2. It was the equivalent of taking off a pair of foggy ski-goggles or glasses.

3. [Did your vision differ ... ?] Different, as my senses seemed to work in an isolated and successive way, not simultaneously. Conscious information therefore seemed more "precise" than usual.

4. I could still see and looked in all directions.

5. Suddenly found myself in the bedroom hovering over the bed looking at the clock and thinking, "Well when you are like this you can see perfectly without your glasses."

6. [Did your vision differ in any way from your normal, everyday vision?] Straight

after I came out of the tunnel I felt as if I was
there but without being there.

7. I thought, "This is Death? How can I see if I
have no eyes?"

8. My realization was that I saw myself from
a new direction, and I watched myself for a
few more moments.

9. The perspective of my memory at that
point changed from looking up at him to
looking down at the top and back of his head
and myself from above.

10. My vision was extremely clear and
intense—as if being in a body was like being
in a lens, and now it was clear.

11. I could see everything. Distance didn't
matter. Everything was so much more real.

List, p. 205.

A Mission to Accomplish in Physical Life.
Said one visitor, "I could now stay with these
beings, or I could take on another assignment
and return to the earth plane." Apparently not
everyone chooses to take on a mission and
physical life. But we are here, and so perhaps we
all have some sort of mission to accomplish.
Perhaps one purpose of it is to progress to a
new stage of personal evolution or spiritual
growth of the higher self.

1. I was told it was not my time and that I
should return to finish my life's work. There
was no negativity about it but a comforting

gesture to return, that I was there by accident.

2. He told me that it was not my time to enter into my heavenly home but had a mission to fulfill and my life was going to be very hard. I would go through many terrible experiences to the point of wanting to commit suicide, but if I committed suicide I would not be allowed to come home. He told me that I would be watched over and protected, kept safe. If I would get through this mission I would be allowed to return home.

3. "I don't want to go back down there; it is painful." "You must! Your mission is not yet complete!"

4. I started arguing with God in my own little obnoxious way, and God said I needed to go back because my mission here wasn't complete.

5. I felt a very strong feeling of depression or failure or something along those lines. This persisted throughout the experience. This is just an interpretation based on subsequent studies of NDEs, but I think it probably had to do with the way I got there (suicide attempt) and the fact that I hadn't completed my mission.

6. I also felt that I had a purpose, a mission that was not yet fulfilled in this life. This was not a work I had to finish, but rather a stage that I had to complete in this life, a form of

spiritual growth.

7. The communication concerned my prenatal chosen human life's work as well as some basic universal laws, which I had overlooked in my human form.

List, p. 241.

"It's Not Your Time": What Does This Mean?
Does it mean a person's date to return home is genetically pre-set? Note last few items on the list.

1. In front of me was something that's hard to describe, almost like an orb or a spirit of some kind. But I heard someone say, "You're not supposed to be here yet. Come with me and go back to your home, it's not your time."

2. Then this Being next to me said that it was time to go now and I will see them again but it was not my time yet. I did not wish to go. I begged to stay and then I felt this dark tight tube around me again, and at this moment I heard the nurse call my name.

3. At this point an unknown, but very clear voice, said to me: "No, you're not going to die, it's really not your time yet (with the implication 'you'll live to be very old') and you're going to get out of this."

4. I was shown a picture through a cloud of my mother dead in the center of the floor with my father, brother and sister crying around her. He told me it was not my time

and that I had to go back for her. After what was shown to me I went down very quickly and found myself in the hospital room with doctors and nurses working on me.

5. I remember feeling very weak when my eyes rolled back into my head. Then suddenly I was standing upright, but not on the ground. It was as if I was floating in a very silent, peaceful space. There was an oval shape of a cloud-like image surrounded in light that became larger and larger in size. I heard a voice saying: "Tina, it is not your time yet, so don't worry or panic." The voice repeated this statement two or three times and then told me to relax, calm my body and concentrate on opening my eyes.

6. I got closer to the light, to the point where the darkness disappeared and I was preparing to join the light. It felt wonderful. Then a loving, caring voice said quite clearly, without words "It's not your time. You must go back." It all disappeared, and at some point after that I regained consciousness.

7. I was greeted with the most handsome spirit who guided me through this experience. I was told it was not my time, but that god wanted me to know to start taking my life more seriously or I would be dead soon. I was told I have to come back and take care of my kids. I was told to be more understanding toward my mother. I also was told he would always be there for

me. I cried because I did not want to come back here because I felt so much peace and calmness and love that I never felt before.

8. I was talking to a lady that said she had to go, but please tell my mother hello for her and that she still thinks of her. I walked her to front door and instead of going out door, she just vanished in front of me. I stood there thinking this isn't a dream ...nothing is out of place but this woman just disappeared in front of me! Then the main lady talking to me said, "It's not your time yet you have to go back." Then she said, "Think about it, you remember," then it was clear at that moment, I said to her, "I'm dead aren't I?" She said, "Yes, but it's not your time yet, you have to go back. You are our go-between." I didn't want to and I proceeded to argue about it.

9. I felt calmer than at any time in my life. I have never felt so at peace or happy. Then my brother came over to me and hugged me and smiled and said it wasn't my time yet. And then all of a sudden I was awake and gasping for breath and surrounded by a whole lot of doctors and nurses.

10. Then I saw this being of light very bright so bright that you could not look at this being. I tried to look but it was much too bright. And this voice said to me, "It's not your time. You have much to learn. Go learn. Don't worry you shall be with me someday.

Go from me now." I didn't want to go but I had no choice in the matter.

11. Then a gentle yet all powerful voice spoke softly to me "Malcolm...Malcolm, it's not your time. Go back now."

12. There is a woman with long dark hair in the light. I am thinking that she is my grandmother only she isn't old anymore. She looks at me and tells me "It's not your time, it just isn't your time."

13. I opened my eyes and saw some villagers trying to help me. I was not sure who they were, and the first thing I asked them was, "Was I alive or dead?" When they told me that I was alive, I again slipped back to unconsciousness, but this time I clearly saw the light and also heard, "It's not your time." Then I woke up.

14. I remember just standing and looking around at this beautiful city so, so beautiful. And when I went around a corner of a building I heard my daughter call me and I was so happy I was going to see her. And then a voice said, "It's not your time yet to be here." And then I woke up.

15. Knowing that I had died seemed totally irrelevant and unimportant. I was not even slightly curious or interested in the body or life I had left behind. While looking for 'the light' within this extremely dark void a voice said to me: 'Go back, it is not your time yet'.

16. On arriving in a very beautiful place, I

was met by my mother who had died two years earlier. She told me this was heaven and began to introduce me to family who had died and I had never known. There was a bright light there that I could not look at because of its brightness. After about twenty minutes a man who I did not know came up and told me, "It's not your time yet and you have to go back."

17. In the background, I could dimly see a group of people and animals that looked like other deceased relatives and pets of mine. My dad spoke and said, "Go back, it's not your time yet."

18. As I got closer and closer to the light, I could feel that I was about to enter into it and I was very excited. I felt that I was about to enter into Heaven. Just then, a lady's voice spoke to me, one of obvious authority. She said, "Don't go into the light. It is not your time yet." I remember bowing my head in disappointment. I awoke out of my coma.

19. I felt that I was about to enter into Heaven. Just then, a lady's voice spoke to me, one of obvious authority. She said, "Don't go into the light. It is not your time yet." I remember bowing my head in disappointment. I awoke out of my coma.

20. Car accident. I remember leaving the scene - moving up a dark tunnel - being pulled slowly by my shoulders. After what seemed like only a few minutes, I stood

suspended in front of two forms of light. The main brightest light form addressed me mentally, saying, "It's not your time yet. You have to go back."

20. I was intent on going into the light but as I was moving toward it I heard him. "What are you doing here?" he asked. "I belong here", I replied. "That I know, but what are you doing here now?" he asked again. A thousand answers were ready to come out of my mouth but before I had time to voice them I knew he was right so I kept my silence and waited. "It is not your time yet", he said in a kind but also firm way. "You still have a lot of work to do".

21. Behind the light I heard a voice that talked to me. I believe I saw my grandmother Susie there. The voice told me that "It's not your time," and that "You'll be there in the end." I was then dismayed that I had to leave. The descent was fast and in the same slanted angle in the tunnel. When I hit bottom it was abrupt and I woke up in severe pain in the recovery room.

22. Suddenly I heard a familiar voice, "Go back Debbie, it's not your time yet!" I immediately recognized this voice as being of my great-grandfather Cecil Collins!

23. There was a gate it looked like shiny hole the room was bright beyond words. I recall feeling peace. No fear and no pain, I was not happy nor was I sad. I felt tranquility. A man

on the other side asked what I wanted. I told him I needed to pass through the gate. He said, "No Don, it isn't your time." I said "But I feel I have to go through!" He again said, "No Don it is not your time yet, go back to your family."

24. My grandmother, who had passed away several years before, was there to greet me. She looked beautiful and there was a light all around her, and also a light all around me. Also, I saw revolving colors that were unlike any that I have ever seen on earth. I asked her: "Am I dead?" She said: "It is not your time, you must go back!" I argued with her and said that I did not want to go back. Then, from a distance, I saw a beautiful and very bright light. I was drawn to it. In this light, I could hear a voice: "You must go back, it is not yet your time. You will recover—you have much work to do." As I protested that I did not want to go back, I shot back into my body faster than the speed of light. After I was back in my body, the pain returned, yet I knew that I would recover and was not afraid.

25. Soon I was before an old man who reminded me of "Father Time." Anyway he had many books that were labeled by planets and by years. The old man looked down on me as he was very large. Compared to my 5' 9" body he must have been 35'! He asked, "What is your name?" I told him my

last name only and he opened up the Book called Earth. Another Book appeared from this one and he opened the years 1900-2000. After gazing in the Book he looked down on me and said; "You must go back it's not your time." I remember the wonderfully beautiful feeling overcoming me and thought, "I don't want to go back." He must have heard my thoughts because he said to me, "You have something to do before you can come here." I asked, "What must I do?" as he said nothing and closed the Book. As soon as the Book closed I awoke in my body again in extreme pain.

26. I said, "Lord will I go home now?" He answered, "No, it is not your time. Your mission is not complete. You have to return."

We Exist in Both Realms At the Same Time. Possibly a person's transcendental or very highest self encompasses their cosmic home and physical life at the same time. Some thought so.

1. I think a part of me is in that light, and I've been only partly here on earth since 1973.

2. It's so apparent, yet we cannot see it while living in the form. At that very moment I likened it to an ant that could never perceive a human in its entirety, its complexity, or its completeness.

3. There is no difference between here and there. They are here but we don't see

them because we are too caught up in the physical world.

4. It is vast. I can't find the words, but there is a message which seems to give me the impression that this place is always here, and is present in all things, and being.

5. [Did you have any sense of altered space or time?] I was definitely in two places at the same time.

List, p. 315.

Some One-of-A-Kind Excerpts. Anomalies can be instructive. And this makes a good place to end this part of the book.

1. Then I walked back, passed the three people and I myself.

2. I then saw a glimpse of my brother and me and somehow seemed to understand it was a previous life, where I was much older than him and was like a mother to him In this life, he is older than me.

3. Then I also saw how my husband's purpose was linked to mine, and how we had decided to come and experience this life together. If I went, he would probably follow soon after. I was made to understand that, as tests had been taken for my organ functions (and the results were not out yet), that if I chose life, the results would show that my organs were functioning normally. If I chose death, the results would show organ failure

as the cause of death, due to cancer. I was able to change the outcome of the tests by my choice!

4. From backward images I saw myself as a young blond-haired young man. I was killed in a car accident and I saw myself leaving the scene with a briefcase walking towards the screen. Before that I saw that I had lived in a suburb in a pale yellow ranch home with a long driveway. Outside the driveway next to the car, I was saying good bye to my wife, my almost-two-year-old daughter, and son about 4 years old. After the kisses and goodbyes I got in my car with my briefcase to go to work.

5. There were small groups of people or spirits (?) in individual rooms called "pods." In these rooms the spirits, or people, were planning their next life or reincarnation.

6. I went back and saw myself in the womb. I was then told to "Remember."

7. I saw three shots of my future. One was my house when I moved in the next months. In the other two, I was old.

8. When I saw myself dead it was my 15-year-old body and all my friends and family looked like they were when I was 15.

9a. He then showed me an image of a young, handsome and wealthy couple that just had a baby boy and he told me that I could be born as that baby.

9b. I was in a new body. New place. A new

life. I had hard time with all of it. I was starting over. ...

9c. The mind is not the person. It's the electricity that makes the body work? ... It's just what I know. Take it as you wish.

9b. I heard farther away someone saying there is a body available, but you must act quick. I said I'll go, but one of the others close to me said, "No, it's too soon for you." I said, "I don't care, I want to go." And they said you must go now or it will be too late. Next thing I remember is being in a crib. And this person was looking at me and talking and smiling. Later I could remember being somewhere inside a wrapping of sorts I would reach to touch it but I couldn't seem to reach it. It was comfortable. But then I would be scared, like claustrophobic.

10. I was unconscious for three weeks, in which I lived another full life. I was 14 again, briefly. (Talk about scary!) The rest was a journey of my TRUE? way. Somehow I got to experience love at first sight and have it returned. I met my husband, Keirin, and we got married in my 'altered' state. My wedding was beautiful, even if it was somewhat rushed. I was not pregnant. Although I recall, we made love and planned to get caught, so that the family would agree to our wedding. The sisters and brothers and the rest of his family were there. My ring was his mother's wedding ring. He asked

me, if his mother's ring was acceptable. I knew it meant so much to him, so of course I said, "Yes." We had calla lilies and white roses everywhere. I'd like to say he wore an afternoon dove-colored tux that would have been time appropriate. But it was a very deep grey/black? I've never seen a man look more wonderful. The most important thing was the feel of his lips right after the ceremony. Loving and hungry, and full of promise, I 'knew' what to expect, but I never ever suspected a man to convey the hope and trust and eagerness of then the present and the future in a breath, in a small moment of time. It was all there: He and I, whatever would be. I have to say that I have never loved, nor given or been loved in that way. In this plane I know of no such person. As a matter of fact, I'm widowed 15 years this year and a second marriage is not on my to-do list. It was all there: He and I, whatever would be. I have to say that I have never loved, nor given or been loved in that way. After I returned to this state I went through a quite normal grieving process at having to leave him behind. I still have a sensation that it wouldn't be unusual at all to turn a street corner and there he'd be. Now that I am here, in this reality, sometimes he is sooooo present here, that I have to turn around to make sure it's here and not there. Considering world events, it feels like I've entered a third reality sometimes. The temptation to return was nearly overwhelming at first. That is not the end of my journey, but what woman in her right mind WOULDN'T want a love such as that. There have been times when the desire is so strong in life I think my heart will break. *[Was the experience dream-like in any way?]* NO. No dream-like quality. It was a contiguous, sequential, and highly understand-able life that made sense. I had no reason to doubt that reality as I was not aware that it was unreal. It is close to two years since the incident and still it is more like memory than a dream.

11. This is what is extraordinary: when the lifeguards were saying that I should be taken to the morgue I could hear them but could not tell them I was alive. I couldn't move or make a signal. I suddenly saw a beautiful, bright light which lighted the place where I was. I looked like a boy eight or nine years old. I was standing in a white robe. Then, two groups of persons appeared dressed as Roman wrestlers; one group was red and the other was blue. They were fighting over me. Both groups wanted to take me and said to each other, "He belongs to us." "No, he belongs here." It looked like they were going to fight with their swords and during that moment of discussion I take the opportunity to run and escape. This is where I get back

my consciousness and started coughing. I immediately got medical attention and am alive to tell you about my Near Death Experience. Lifeguards said it was a miracle: "We thought you were dead and we were taking you to the morgue."

"Not Supposed To": Rules and Enforcement

1. We are not supposed to take our own life. I was fully aware of what I had done and the thought of being alone in that nothing forever was unbearable but what could I do? It was too late. Suddenly in the void I heard a voice, a male voice, and He said, "It's o.k. It's all right. It's all good."

2. When the person reached me we spoke through thought. He told me that it was not my time to enter into my heavenly home but had a mission to fulfill and my life was going to be very hard. I would go through many terrible experiences to the point of wanting to commit suicide, but if I committed suicide I would not be allowed to come home.

3. I was allowed to make the decision whether or not to return.

4. I wanted to go to the "sun" but someone telepathically told me I couldn't. I thought that I was awake and that my body was still in this world, so I stopped for a moment and wondered why the "sun" attracted me so, and why I couldn't go towards it. But at the

same time I knew, I don't know how, that I wasn't allowed to go to the "sun." So I decided to disobey that voice inside of me that told me I couldn't because the attraction was really too great. Then in a fraction of a second, as I was attempting to go towards that light, I was projected into my body and I heard some people who were telling me to throw up the water.

5. We get to this enormous light and I feel that my companion gets there before me, and I just know it's a boy my age: 17 years. We are greeted by a "being" that is light, it's like a glow coming from it. I don't know if it's a she or a he. But it radiates so much love and safety it's indescribable. The boy "disappears" into the light, but for some reason I'm not allowed to come along. I so much want to come too, it's so wonderfully comfortable. I feel so absolutely great. I stay by the light being, I can't get past it. I'm told it's not my time yet. Then everything goes black. When I woke up later I felt such an enormous sense of loss and disappointment because I couldn't go too. I'm almost angry about it.

6. [Did you have a sense of knowing special knowledge, universal order and/or purpose?] Yes, I feel that when death comes close, this one, death, allows you to choose whether you want to go or stay.

7. I remembered that I had a daughter, and

before I could plead my case for returning, I was told by thought that I would not be allowed to stay. I got excited to return, and thought how much I wanted to remember the knowledge, so I could explain it to others, ease fears of death, and inspire goodness.

8. I was born a "totally awake" psychic. I saw and spoke with supposedly "dead people", including the being known as Jesus, all of my life. I meditated regularly, and prayed regularly. I was accustomed to being out of my body frequently while doing this. I think this is why there was no "tunnel/white light" in my experience. I was already familiar with and comfortable on the "other side". Suddenly I was in a round Greek style temple that was not roofed. Jesus was before me and I was aware that there were 70 other people there to work with me. There was a mist that hid their faces from me, though I could see Jesus quite clearly. I was aware that each of them was working with me in my soul's growth and various karmic matters I had elected to work on during this body's sojourn. Jesus informed me that I had completed the work I had come in to do, and had "channeled" the 3 souls who would affect the future <my>. I could now stay with these beings, or I could take on another assignment and return to the earth plane. I don't usually make hasty

decisions, and "he" knew that. I told him that was ridiculous. I would need time to consider the pros and cons of both scenarios, and that earthly body wasn't going to last for long. He laughed, snapped his fingers and my three children were standing before. I instantly knew that I had the "keys" that would unlock their memories when it was time for them to awaken, but that their father did not. If I opted to stay, they would have to come into the body again in another life to fulfill their destinies. I look at Jesus and said, "That's really unfair!! You know I can't leave them to come back again. This is emotional blackmail!" At which he cocked and eyebrow at me and laughed again. Then he responded, "But you do want them to succeed this time, don't you?" I replied, "Yes, you know I do. But I have a condition. If I go back, I want to be allowed to heal people. Not just their bodies, but their souls too. I want to awaken them to their soul's potential and Truth." Jesus smiled and answered, "As you desire, so shall it be." I awakened to my anesthesiologist cursing up a storm.

9. Then she saw IT, the music and colors that were indescribably beautiful and a light with such an intense beauty and mildness as never before. She was not allowed to go through.

10. I felt that I was about to enter into Heaven. Just then, a lady's voice spoke to me, one of obvious authority. She said, "Don't go into the light. It is not your time yet." I remember bowing my head in disappointment. I awoke out of my coma.

List, p. 209

FULL LISTS OF SIMILAR EXCERPTS

CONSCIOUSNESS CONTINUED FOR ALL

1. I was conscious of "being me" throughout. (Each number indicates a different visitor/eye witness.)

2. I could move around, in short I had an "I."

3. All the time I was also aware of my body and I was watching what was happening to it.

4. I was more alive than I had ever been before.

5. Throughout the period the self-level of consciousness and alertness was there.

6. I felt that my body was separate from my spirit and they were on two different planes of existence.

7. During the experience I seemed to be perfectly lucid and conscious.

8. I had departed from my physical body and was looking at my hospital room from the corner of the ceiling.

9. And I sure was OK, felt great, full of a sensation of fulfillment, and conscious of what had happened to me.

10. I believe I was conscious throughout the whole event.

11. My whole self was like a sole consciousness – no body, no extension, no beginning and no end in that awareness that was me.

12. I was fully conscious of everything, feeling and thinking very clearly

13. I was free, the world of pain had disappeared, I was more focused.

14. [Did you experience a separation of your

consciousness from your body?] Yes.

15. I saw and felt with great clarity.

16. The next thing I saw was my body below me. But to me it wasn't me because I was here above this body that was mine.

17. I was fully conscious of being outside my body.

18. It was me but not in my body.

19. I remember saying to myself, "I am all right," out loud to my self. ... I was me looking down but was not Bob. I did not even know Bob, but I was still me as I was before I drowned. I do not know how to explain this any other way.

20. I was just "Myself" for whatever that means.

21. I was pure consciousness having/retaining all knowledge of my life and memories. I was not any smarter.

22. My conscience was connected to a translucent body.

23. I was fully aware of who I am.

24. You are very much awake after you die, and very much alert.

25. I found myself outside my body as a transparent and weightless me.

26. At that moment, I started to walk away from myself. My vision was clear. My person, my body, was moving away from me. I reached out and tried to grab myself. My hand swept through me as if there was nothing there.

27. I was aware of four states of consciousness: awake, dreaming, hallucinating, and out of body in another realm.

28. At one point instead of losing consciousness, I was very present and very aware of being.

29. I still remained conscious. My senses were tremendously alert.

30. I could sense myself in the outline form of my body but my body wasn't there.

31. I had been examining my hands and arms, which were a translucent light blue. I still looked normal, but without actual body mass..

32. My experience consisted of becoming consciously aware of floating above my body.

33. I experienced this incredibly intense and calm state of awareness. There was no drifting of consciousness as in the normal living state. It was an all-consuming state of awareness.

THINKING BECAME MORE POWERFUL

1. I felt as though I had been liberated from my body, and being outside my body freed me from the limitations imposed by a physical existence. My mind felt cleared and my thoughts seemed quick and decisive.

2. I kept on THINKING.

3. I was seeing, feeling, but I had a body that looked like transparent! But my thinking was normal.

4. I also understood that my body is like a car my consciousness drives.

5. For a while I ceased to exist, then darkness, a clear sensation of floating during which my mind continued to function.

6. I was so confused thinking, "Wow! Why do they bother? I don't need my body. I'm fine, actually better than before."

7. When I was "in" my body, I didn't know what was going on. When I was "hovering" I had vivid thoughts.

8. I felt that my body was separate from my spirit and they were on two different planes of existence.

9. During the experience I seemed to be perfectly lucid and conscious.

10. I remember just thinking: "No. Where am I? Where are we going?"

11. I remember thinking, "That was cool being Thomas," like it was some fun excursion, this human life.

12. I knew what was going on. I knew it as a fact, not assuming. I was dead.

13. I remember being able to think and figure out what do, figure out all the outcomes.

14. In my mind I asked what was happening.

15. I thought about my two grown sons, neither of whom I had told about the surgery. It was an indifferent, wondering feeling to think how surprised they would be to learn I was dead. [What emotions did you feel during the experience?] Detachment from family, peace, relief.

16. And I sure was OK, felt great, full of a sensation of fulfillment, and conscious of what had happened to me.

17. I thought that I was awake and that my body was still in this world, so I stopped for a moment and wondered why the "sun" attracted me so, and why I couldn't go towards it. But at the same time I knew, I don't know how, that I wasn't allowed to go to the "sun."

18. I remember thinking that I was not prepared to die...too young.

19. I tried to say, "No! Don't hurt him. Leave him alone." I realized it seemed a bit strange to refer to myself as "him," but at that time, I felt that I was the entity looking down on a man who looked a lot like I used to look but that it wasn't really me.

20. I was fully conscious of everything, feeling and thinking very clearly.

21. I was told all my thoughts were in the

past; that none of that mattered anymore. It was so peaceful.

22. I remember saying to myself, "I am all right," out loud to my self. ... I was me looking down but was not Bob. I did not even know Bob, but I was still me as I was before I drowned. I do not know how to explain this any other way. I believe that our bodies die but we do live on

23. I thought, "Hey what's going on? That's me down there?"

24. I was aware of my state. I was surely going somewhere, but where I did not know.

25. But I'm still aware! I was very aware. ... I was more like thought in space, completely alone in nothingness.

26. I didn't have a body. I was immaterial. I had only my thought and stop, nothing all. I forgot my body.

27. Everything slowed down that I saw, but my thoughts sped up simultaneously.

28. I had no other thoughts other than wanting to go on towards the light.

29. I thought, "Omg, I'm dead and they are going to bury me, but I'm not dead. I can see them and myself!" My next thought was, "I'm too young to die!"

30. I found I could think clearly with no distractions.

31. I asked myself a couple of times in succession, "How can I be doing this?" The answer was too obvious. "I must be dead!" I told myself.

32. I remember thinking it was nice to have no

worries, no pain, fear etc.

33. It was death and knowing I was dead. ... I was wondering why I died. What happened? And thinking it must have been a fast death.

34. I am thinking, "Where am I?" At first I tell myself I must be dreaming. I think I am in a movie theater. It is so dark I can see nothing. Sounds crazy I know, but then I realize or I am thinking I have died.

35. My mind was somewhere outside the body. ... You are very much awake after you die, and very much alert.

36. In my mind, I thought for sure I was dying.

37. Suddenly I was thinking: "What does it all matter? I want to go there now, experience something else..."

38. I thought to myself, "I am supposed to be dead right this very instant." I felt as if I was looking down to my left, in my mind's eye that is. I

39. Just as I realized that was my lifeless body in the bed below, my thoughts were abruptly distracted.

40. Was cussing myself out, thinking I must of OD'd; now I'm dead.

41. I was pulled into a tunnel. I remember thinking, "I'm dying, I'm dying!"

42. While being in this void I also knew (?) that I was dead and needed to look for 'the light'.

43. I remember thinking that I didn't want to die yet.

44. I began to drift and realize I was not inside of

my body.

45. I just slid out of my body and rose above the bed and said to myself, "I thought this one was supposed to be longer."

46. My thinking process was also different, more lucid and rapid than in physical existence. My mind and attention span were so amazingly clear that I could easily understand what I was told.

47. I spent some time thinking about the life that went with those feelings. Not exactly judging, but measuring foul-ups against successes.

48. My life's history exploded into my consciousness. I thought I wasn't ready to go yet, I had more things to accomplish in this life, and I wanted another chance to do the things I needed to do.

49. I remember thinking that I had no pain and questioning why I couldn't feel any pain. I knew I wasn't in my body, but it didn't feel like I was without a body.

50. I remember thinking, "Yes, this is the birth canal," I thought with a big sigh, "I don't want to be born again." I realized with relief that wasn't happening.

51. I then began to have a dialogue with myself, not moving my lips but talking in my brain.

52. The thought that, "This is what death is all about." kept recurring in my mind over and over.

53. I remember thinking I must be dead. I couldn't feel my body—don't think I had one,

but I was still me with crystal clear thinking.

54. I took the fact that I didn't have a body meant that my body would never work again. I decided to go on to die.

55. There I was dead, but my mind was so very much alive.

56. My world ceased to exist, except for my mind.

57. I have no recollection of having any type of form, just thought.

58. What jolted me was the thought, "What about my family?"

59. I had the mental state as though I knew I was going to die and was okay with it.

60. I thought, "Why aren't they listening to me?"

61. I'm me the way I was a moment before, no change. ... As I was floating I found myself thinking of my life.

62. There were full powers of logical reasoning and language.

63. I was pure thought flowing in a wondrous river of peace and loving feeling.

64. I vividly recall floating/hovering above myself and thinking: "What am I doing up here?"

65. I remember thinking, "I wonder if I've died?"

66. I remember thinking. It was more like knowing instead of thinking.

67. I kept thinking at every turn that this was wonderful and amazing.

68. I'm still wondering, "What is happening to me?"

69. I did not have any physical sensations, but I could think and communicate.

70. There was no discontinuity of consciousness. My first thought was, "Well, I guess this is what it's like to be dead."

71. In my head I just kept saying that this was unbelievably fantastic and surprising.

72. The time moved fast and I thought very fast.

73. I was pure intellect, absorbing information and knowledge through "sensors" or means that I have no concept of..

74. [At what time during the experience were you at your highest level of consciousness and alertness?] I was conscious during this time, but I cannot control my thoughts.

75. I felt this incredible power to devote my total concentration on several different things at the same time.

PERSONS INHABIT THE AFTERLIFE

1. While in the boat, the person took off his hood and revealed a man I call "Santa Claus."

2. This person got up and came down the stairs and down the road to me. ... When the person reached me we spoke through thought.

3. When I told the truth I got to go on to the next person.

4. [Did you see or visit any beautiful or otherwise distinctive locations, levels or dimensions?] Heaven or a beautiful field that people were there with all kinds of animals.

4. There was someone on my right holding my arm taking me. I could tell that this person KNEW where we were going and it was their mission to bring me.

5. I was standing on a beach naked, approx. 20 feet in front of me was another naked person, in front of him/her at the same distance another and so forth. ... Beside me in both directions at about 20 feet were other people, and beside them others. ... We were all naked and unmoving, unable to speak—only hear and see. The beach was endless. The most captivating part of this was that there was an ocean with waves crashing in over people who were unable to move, and then receding to show that person was still there. ... Then to my right I noticed that there was someone moving freely, not walking but just appearing in front of some of the people there. I had noticed this person from a long way off as he

seemed very small, just an silhouette. Then he was in front of me.

6. And this person was looking at me and talking and smiling.

7. I didn't see the face of the person I was walking with, nevertheless he wore a white tunic and I walked on his left.

8. At this time I was being pulled at a high rate of speed and there was somebody with me and I felt safe and loved and at peace. This person was transparent but I could still see him smiling at me and saying to me, but not talking with his mouth but his mind, telling me, "Every thing is fine."

9. I was asked by a person who's image was blurred, "Do you want to return?"

10. On top of the table was a book in front of the person that was directly to my left.

11. My spirit person was screaming and trying to wake up my mom, but she couldn't hear me.

12. ... I realized that the person I saw was not a man but an Angel ... .

13. Don't know how long I was in the light. The light was instant to me. I opened my eyes. I was lying on someone's lap. Wondering who this person is, where am I? I was in a new body. New place. A new life. I had hard time with all of it.

14. The person beside me put out his hand over my crossed hands on my chest and said to me, "You have to go back, your time is not yet." At this time I was being pulled at a high rate of

speed and there was somebody with me and I felt safe and loved and at peace. This person was transparent but I could still see him smiling at me and saying to me, but not talking with his mouth but his mind, telling me, "Everything is fine."

15. One night while asleep in 1992 I saw my deceased friend while I was out of my body in a room that had rows of church-pew-style seats. There was another person there, a male. He was holding out a white coat towards me saying if I wanted to be with her then I had to put it on.

16. I began to "see" a progression of past lives. These were usually from the dual point of view of the person whose life I was viewing and from my own present perspective.

17. There was a figure off to the left side of this door. To me it looked transparent, the color of liquid coffee held up to the light. It was the shape of a tall, thin person in a long, hooded robe. It seemed more transparent in what would be the chest area and I could not see a face or any detailed features.

18. I could feel someone on both sides of me, and we were approaching this person with two other persons on each side of that person. I felt as though this person was both male and female. As I got closer I could see white. Each person on the sides was very important to the person in the middle, and there was love. The person in the middle had on a bright white robe, and I remember seeing gold ropes hanging from the

waist of this person, but I could never see a face. As I approached and stood in front of this person I felt incredible love. I did not want to leave, but I could hear this person say, "Breathe." Just as this was said to me, I took a deep breath and woke up.

19. The focus of the experience, however, was on a well-dressed professional looking man standing before me and apparently communicating with me. (Although I don't believe that there was any verbal communication, there was perfect understanding.) The person wore a white shirt and necktie, and appeared as some one who had just removed his suit coat. The entire scene had the impression of informality, but yet being very important. This person seemed to be using a blackboard and white chalk as an aid to his delivery. The most apt way that I have found to convey my overall impression is to liken it to an orientation session for some corporation/business. I remember distinctly trying, during the experience, to put it into proper context. I told myself that I was "dreaming" but, as if arguing with myself, saying, "No, this is entirely too real to be a dream."

20. During this, I felt as if I was two people; I think that's the best way to put it. It was as if one person was lying on the trolley and one was sitting up, but both trying to work together simultaneously. I could see my arms and legs, but it felt like I was inside a large boiler suit.

21. I could see a person inside the light. The light was bright, but not glaring. It did not dazzle the eyes. It got close enough for me to look at what was inside. There was a very soothing, very strong, but not overbearing thought in my mind that said, "Childing, do not be afraid. We will not harm you in any way."

22. On my left side, I view people walking two by two in a very calm way. One is a person who crossed; the other is their guide.

23. The person who was watching me walked across the bridge and said goodbye to me. I was too young to understand what had happened and didn't think much about it until years later.

24. I was thinking of a lady that was incredibly happy on earth, and I was certain that she should be around here. Out of the blue before I could finish my thought there she was walking past me only 10 times happier. I just thought of the particular person and right there they appear in front of me.

25. Then she had an experience like traveling through a dark tunnel, seeing to the right of the end of the tunnel a female person, dressed in white, with dark hair.

26. This light was a person! I never saw a face however I had the knowledge or inner vision of a face. This face was smiling and very happy to see me. The peace was not to imagine. Then I knew what this person was saying: "I Love You."

27. My experience was this: I realized I was in a very bright office with a man in white standing at

my side and an administrative type, all in white, at a desk. This person began to ask me many questions about my life. I knew I was very ill and the minute I thought, "WHY is he wasting time asking me all these questions?" The other person began pushing me on a gurney down a long hallway. I got up & began to walk along beside the gurney & suddenly realized that half of my body was walking 'through' the wall.

28. I seemed to follow a particular person, followed his progress in heaven, immediately at and after he died! I was right by his side as IF I WERE that person in an "autobiography" of months of living there. So I will use the first person "I" here as if I WERE that person in order to simplify things!

29. A person or St. Peter-like thing said I couldn't go into the light until I decided if I wanted to stay.

30. The Divine Being looked upon him and asked how he came to be there. He replied that a person in white raiment had come to him and brought him to this glorious place. The Divine Being told the Guide to take John and show him the glory of the Saints.

31. I could see myself lying on the bed. There was somebody beside me, but I couldn't see a face. I wasn't frightened of him. I saw the doctor who was stitching my head turn to the other doctor, say something, then I saw him put his hand in his top pocket. Then I was in another room, with the person still beside me. We were facing a door that was open where inside was a

man, he turned towards me and I could see two small round red indentations either side of his head just above the temples.

32. I saw people that I would have been repulsed by or impressed by when looking at them from a lower awareness. But in that higher view I actually saw that they were made out of The Light. It wasn't physical light, which is limited to the physical dimensions, but Real Light, multidimensional, spiritual.

33. I could clearly see that they were human, but in this existence were beings of light. They seemed to be the same colour as the electric blue in the first tunnel. I was greeted with a great love and urgency. I was held, and knowledge was imbued into me. I was told, this is not my time, but this was meant to happen.

34. The Person who first welcomed me came and placed his hand on my shoulder and turned me towards Him. He said, "You must return, you have a task to perform."

35. There were a lot of people with me and we were trying to escape from it but could not.

36. Next there was a field on the right with people working in it harvesting some kind of grain.

37. There were small groups of people or spirits(?) in individual rooms called "pods." In these rooms the spirits or people were planning their next life or reincarnation.

38. There were three "people" behind the curtain and they seemed unsure about letting me in. I

couldn't see what they looked like, just vague images behind the curtain. Then one of them told me, "It's not time yet, go back."

39. He was told God sends us people to help us get to heaven.

40. I had noticed this person from a long way off as he seemed very small, just a silhouette. Then he was in front of me.

41. I continued on with a (person, spirit being) dressed in a monk's gown.

42. Eventually the tunnel let out onto a platform with a marble floor. There were various people milling about in grey hooded robes. One of them came up to me and introduced himself as my guide.

DECEASED FAMILY AND FRIENDS THERE

1. [Did you meet or see any other beings?] Yes, my grandmother. I did not see her but I knew it was her for some reason which I cannot explain.

2. I remember my uncle, my aunt, and my grandma and grandpa were waiting for me when I went through the white light.

3. Every member of my family and friends who had died was there. Even my dogs. ... Then my brother came over to me and hugged me and smiled and said it wasn't my time yet.

4. My sister, who had passed away 21 years before my experience, she was doing some type of work with other beings, who had human form, but I do not remember their faces.

5. I remember my Dad sitting on a stoop of sorts with his hand outstretched to me. He was many years younger than he was when he died, and I was just a toddler reaching up to him. I know I saw lots of people, but can't remember who they were specifically, except for my Dad.

6. My mother, who had died only a short time before this, was explaining to me what was going on and had told me that I was going to be just fine. She said this had to be done so she could properly explain to me what had happened to her. ... She then explained to me that I would not see her for a while, but that she would always be with me. ... She then gave me a big hug and kiss and the brightest light I ever seen (without

squinting not one bit) appeared and she walked to it and before she disappeared she said, "I love you and be a good boy."

7. [Did you meet or see any other beings?] Yes. They were at the end of the tunnel. I knew one but I did not see the others clearly. The one I knew was my brother. He told me to do not cry any more for him, that he died because it was his time and that he was taking care of me from that dimension.

8. [Did you hear any unusual sounds or noises?] Yes, steady vector, air sounds like loud jet engines without the hurting effect on my ears, and a voice of people, my dead grandparents, friends, and past historians ...

9. Then in a commanding voice, she said, "You must go back now." I turned to look at her. It was my mother. Since her death, I always dreamed of her pale with bed sores and bandages, but this time it was different. It was the first time I had seen her looking so young and healthy. Mother looked like a beautiful twenty-two-year-old woman with a perfect body.

10. I also saw my parents, deceased in 1979, making signs in order to invite me to follow them. . I saw silhouettes of sorts and sensed that it was my mother who died in 1971, my friend who died in 1976, and my grandfather who died in 1979. I wanted to go to them but heard from them, "No, not yet." I was disappointed and angry as I wanted to see them, especially my mom.

11. I was with my biological mother who passed

12 yrs earlier and countless others who loved me and were so happy to see me and I them.

12. She said that she recognized my grandfather, her mother and father, her brothers, and several other family members, but then an angel of unspeakable beauty stopped her as she headed toward them.

13. Rose up in a ray of light, until I was asked, "Do you believe in God?" I answered, "Yes," and had to leave the light. It was light blue all around me, and I saw my grandmother in an old boat, rather upset at the fact I was a believer.

14. I was in another land. The most wonderful and beautiful place I have ever seen. ... I met people and we just knew everything. We exchanged smiles and I said I was looking for my sister and daughter. I knew they were there, it was just a matter of finding them.

15. I do remember being with three others, one in the middle was a little above the two, on one side was my brother, who died at 11days, the other was my grandpa.

16. Then, I realized that the person in front was my beloved Uncle, my closest deceased relative, and behind him was my grandmother, his mother.

17. I saw silhouettes of sorts and sensed that it was my mother who died in 1971, my friend who died in 1976, and my grandfather who died in 1979. I wanted to go to them but heard from them, "No, not yet." I was disappointed and angry as I wanted to see them, especially my mom.

18. Then all of a sudden I saw all my (deceased) family members come towards me.

19. Then I saw above me, my grandfather who had died when I was probably in my teens. He had a boxer dog on a leash with him which somehow I knew was part of my grandfather's family.

20. As I got to the end of the tunnel and I was bathed in warm sunlight, the sky above me became dark, with only bits of light getting through. The darkness was caused by my family, friends, and a pet...all of whom had died before me. They were hovering over me. I was standing looking up at them above me. Each person/animal moved to create a human chain to block the light from reaching me. My father's voice spoke to me. He said that I was okay, safe, and had a choice. He said that I could come to them or I could stay where I was and continue with my "earthly" life. Each time a beam or glint of light came on or near, my grandfather, grandmother, past partner, friends who had died of AIDS, and dog (a beautiful Bichon) would all shift to block the bright light.

21. I am out of my body looking at the paramedics who do not seem to be doing anything. I see myself and it is blurry. Then I am back in my body, and at my feet is my younger brother who had died years before of cancer at the age of thirty. He is shaking his head as if to say, "No, no it is not your time." ... On my brother's shoulder is a bird. I look closer and it is

my bird Doolittle the parakeet.

22. On the other side I saw my great grandfathers, one from peacetime born in 1865, and the other from the civil war in a tattered gray uniform. I saw one who was a state senator.

23. I believe I saw my grandmother Susie there.

24. I saw my Dad all in white and what looked like a soft robe on. My Mother was next to him, and my Mother's parents were next to her.

25. Then I saw above me, my grandfather who had died when I was probably in my teens.

26. The second, was my uncle who died back 1975, it wasn't his body, but for some reason I knew it was him. The third was my kids' grandfather who died early that year.

27. In the light my father started to appear to me and seemed to hold out his hand, as if to motion me to come with him.

28. [Did you meet or see any other beings?] My family who had died severely painful deaths.

29. [Did you meet or see any other beings?] Yes, just saw the face of my deceased uncle and a friend who died at a young age.

30. There in front of me stood my father. My dad had died on Christmas Eve of 1998

31. My mother then looked at me and said, but not in words only in thought, "You have been given a second chance. I can take you the rest of the way, or you can go back."

32. I glanced back at Granddad and was propelled quickly towards the entrance.

32. He explained that he was there as my father

of my family tree, that I was his great x many grand daughter.

33. He saw his brother-in-law that passed away about a year before.

34. I could hear my family and see them, but they couldn't see me.

35. There is a woman with long dark hair in the light. I am thinking that she is my grandmother only she isn't old anymore.

36. My Father died when I was 11 years old, and I sensed his presence.

37. I immediately recognized this voice as being of my great-grandfather Cecil!

38. And then I saw my Mom, who is deceased.

39. My grandfather was looking up to Him.

40. I heard my grandmother calling me and asking me what I am doing 'here'.

41. The darkness was caused by my family, friends, and a pet...all of whom had died before me.

42. I know I saw my dad who has been dead for many years

43. I heard my daughter call me and I was so happy I was going to see her ...

44. ... my nephews, grandparents, aunt and lots of others.

45. As I was about to go into the light with even a more wonderful feeling, I noticed something below me and to the right. As I glanced over I noticed it was my mother's father who died years earlier looking at me waving his arms in a do not enter movement so I stopped in my tracks, like

superman can do in his movies, and stared at my grandfather.

46. A vast mile-sized building called, they told me, "The Veteran's Reuniting Center" (I think) where the people who just arrived after dying can find and meet their relatives/friends, who died before them. But this building could also be a center for veteran's of earth's wars! I saw a whole group of spirits progress onto a higher heaven.

47. I then saw a glimpse of my brother and me and somehow seemed to understand it was a previous life, where I was much older than him and was like a mother to him (in this life, he is older than me). I saw in that life I was very protective towards him. I suddenly became aware he was on the plane to come and see me, and felt, "I can't do this to him—can't let him come and see me dead".

48. I could hear the doctor saying, "Don't, don't, no, no." The next thing I know I was floating up and through the ceiling and into space. I came into a large room full of light and then my eyes adjusted and I recognized my grandmother and friends and other family members.

49. I remember feeling the presence of my deceased Father in the distance.

50. My mother, who had died only a short time before this, was explaining to me what was going on and had told me that I was going to be just fine. She said this had to be done so she could properly explain to me what had happened to

her.

51. I heard people talking downstairs and I got up to see who it was. As I confronted them all hanging out on couch and kitchen table. They started saying hello and talking to me. I knew by the southern accent they must be relatives but I didn't know who... but as I looked around I started thinking they looked like people I knew that were dead. They kept visiting. I was talking to a lady that said she had to go, but please tell my mother hello for her and that she still thinks of her.

52. I suddenly felt the presence of intense comfort and love, then my grandmother and her mother (I had never met), both Native Americans. They told me that it was not my time. (I didn't hear them I just knew it.) They were there to give me strength.

53. When I reached again the light I went through it again and I saw my brother (he died 4 years ago). I hugged him and after crying for some minutes he looked at me and told me that I had not to cry for his death.

54. On arriving in a very beautiful place, I was met by my mother who had died two years earlier. She told me this was heaven and began to introduce me to family who had died and I had never known.

LIGHT PERSONS AND THE PERSON IN THE LIGHT

1. I saw an immense, central light at the end of the path. It was as if a superior being was seated at the end, very luminous. Additionally, he interrogated me about why I was in that place.

2. ... and the warm light was "God" or my idea of God - I felt loved and cared for and precious - which was fabulous ...

3. The light is becoming brighter and larger, and all I can feel is the presence of good, and now am sure this is where I need to be. Finally, the end of the tunnel is here, and I am enveloped in that same light, that without a word spoken, directed me here.

4. I got closer to the light, to the point where the darkness disappeared and I was preparing to join the light. It felt wonderful. Then a loving, caring voice said quite clearly, without words, "It's not your time. You must go back." [Did you see a light?] It was blinding, but out of it radiated the most wondrous feelings of love, peace and joy. I couldn't wait to join it.

5. I saw a figure of light come towards me out of the light. This figure was very tall. I am guessing it was about 8 feet tall or so. I am saying "it" because I could not tell if it was male or female. The "being" spoke to me although the words were not heard with my

ears. It was as if someone was speaking in my head, although it was not my voice I heard. Everything was so crystal clear and seemed to make perfect sense although logically it was impossible. The figure told me "You must go back, we are not ready for you yet."

6. Then a bright light appeared having a soft man's voice ... . The light also gave me an important message to follow it as much possible.

7. [Had two nde's.] On both occasions a being of white light appeared to me and took my hand and took me to a door that opened on its own.

8. There was an oval shape of a cloud-like image surrounded in light that became larger and larger in size. I heard a voice saying; "Tina, it is not your time yet, so don't worry or panic." The voice repeated this statement two or three times and then told me to relax, calm my body and concentrate on opening my eyes.

9. At one point I became aware of a light that was with me that I'll refer to as a presence. The presence was communicating with me, and assuring me I was safe, and led me through a beautiful field with flowers and trees and a creek. The presence was telling me I would no longer have any worries or troubles, and was so calming.

10. And in the distance I saw a glowing point

light up. While I was watching it became bigger, like the sun rising and it came through the closed window into the room and embraced me completely.

11. [At what time during the experience were you at your highest level of consciousness and alertness?] When I met the human-like being in the light.

12. I was obedient to the light and noise which told me to wake.

13. Then a moment came when I was brought up short by a "wall" of dense light, which gave off an unbelievable goodness, an indescribable love. And I heard a voice filled with tenderness say to me: "It's not time, you must go back, it's much too soon." [Did you meet or see any other beings?] Yes, precisely this light, which was living.

14. We are greeted by a "being" that is light, it's like a glow coming from it. I don't know if it's a she or a he. But it radiates so much love and safety it's indescribable. ... I stay by the light being, I can't get past it. I'm told it's not my time yet.

15. I just recall being drawn towards a big bright light to the point where I was in the light, only to have it communicated (somehow) that it was time to leave and back I came.

16. The light was pulsating as if alive.

17. Then this awesome light exploded in front of me and I stood in that light and I felt

wonderful. It seemed to heal everything, and I can't remember all of what it said, but if you asked a question in it it would answer you before you could think of it.

18. [Did you see a light?] A bright, intense light that felt so warm and good, so loving and full of wisdom.

19. Then I saw this being of light very bright so bright that you could not look at this being. I tried to look but it was much too bright. And this voice said to me, "It's not your time." "You have much to learn, go learn." "Don't worry you shall be with me someday. Go from me now."

20. I saw a light and I went into it. It was wondrous light that engulfed everything, there was total knowledge and love. I saw my life from my addiction point of view flash before my eyes, repeated behaviors etc. ... I was then told to "Remember."

21. I went towards this presence, which was within a brilliant, sun-light bright, light space.

22. I was being pulled into a white Light. I wanted to get there as quickly as possible, because all of these wonderful, ecstatic, feelings emanating from this Light: UNCONDITIONAL LOVE, FORGIVENESS, EMPATHY, COMPLETE ACCEPTANCE OF ME, DEEP UNDERSTANDING.

23. I could see a person inside the light. The light was bright, but not glaring. It did not

dazzle the eyes. It got close enough for me to look at what was inside. There was a very soothing, very strong, but not overbearing thought in my mind that said, "Childing, do not be afraid. We will not harm you in any way."

24. I was instantly surrounded by the most beautiful, pure light and colors that cannot even be imagined. The light was everywhere and went into me. I felt pure love, acceptance, and perfect happiness.

25. I could clearly see that they were human, but in this existence were beings of light. They seemed to be the same colour as the electric blue in the first tunnel. I was greeted with a great love and urgency. I was held, and knowledge was imbued into me. I was told, this is not my time, but this was

26. I was traveling in the light at an amazing speed/absorption where I came to this space, open space of light and I could see all of these images of people outlined in light. There were no clothes on anyone, and I could not make out faces as male or female. There were no boundaries; it was as open as the eye could see and I could see images of people and their forms as far as I could see. I instantly had no fear. I was filled with love and peace that I can only describe and can never do it justice. I was so loved and accepted. I had never felt so loved in all my life. The peace, serenity, joy, and no pain was

unbelievable!

27. I was engulfed in a beautiful light. It was all around me and it was composed of unimaginable kindness. It was like being in the middle of the sun. I delighted the sun. It knew what I was like, faults and all, but it loved me completely.

28. As I approached the light it spoke to me telepathically. With each word the the light brightened and dimmed rhythmically. At first he kind of scolded me and asked what I was doing there as it wasn't my time yet. I had to go back. I was apologetic and very disappointed.

29. I stood suspended in front of two forms of light. The main brightest light form addressed me mentally, saying ... "It's not your time yet —you have to go back."

30. The light became much brighter and there was a warmth and sense of well-being that I can only describe as ultimate peacefulness. Behind the light I heard a voice that talked to me.

31. I was in so much bliss going toward the light. The feelings I felt were so loving and peaceful, nothing like I ever felt on earth.

32. When I had totally slipped away, I felt bathed in a wonderful light, as though I was being hugged by it. I felt totally safe, that all was forgiven, and I was very, very loved.

33. This light was a person! I never saw a face, however I had the knowledge or inner

vision of a face. This face was smiling and very happy to see me. The peace was not to imagine. Then I knew what this person was saying: "I Love You."

34. I screeched with the fear of meeting the being in the light.

35. ... I found myself back at the entrance to the room of the beings of light. Something felt wrong; I wondered what had happened. I felt a presence of my former guide meeting another entity in front of the beings of lights choir stand. They seemed to be having a disagreement about something; I had hoped that it was not about my being here. I couldn't tell exactly what the problem was but I sensed there was a very serious one. I had the sense that I was being brought back to life ... .

36. Then I encountered beings of Light whom I called my Angels. It was awesome. They told me: "You're okay. Everything is okay. Don't worry." And I knew it. Then I woke up several days later, and the nurse and the surgeons could not believe it. I heard them say: "It's a Miracle!"

37. Then, I saw many beings of light waiting for me and saying, "Welcome back." They were happy to see me again and they were welcoming and radiating all their love to me.

38. 1. Bha was talking animatedly with a blue light being; he was tall and the shape of a man, but he had no features. A neon

turquoise blue light outlined his shape and he had lights moving on the inside of his shape like sunlight playing on water.

39. Suddenly, I turned around and I came face to face with this light being who looked human. As I looked around there were millions of light humanoid creatures all over the place.

40. We get to this enormous light and I feel that my companion gets there before me, and I just know it's a boy my age: 17 years. We are greeted by a "being" that is light, it's like a glow coming from it. I don't know if it's a she or a he. But it radiates so much love and safety it's indescribable. The boy "disappears" into the light, but for some reason I'm not allowed to come along. I so much want to come too, it's so wonderfully comfortable. I feel so absolutely great. I stay by the light being, I can't get past it. I'm told it's not my time yet. Then everything goes black.

AFTERLIFE FILLED WITH LOVE

1. I came into the light. The light was so brilliant but neither warm nor cold. It was almost as if it consumed me. A feeling of Love so powerful and consuming, washed over me.

2. I saw people on this Seashore and I seem to know these people even though I have never seen them in this dimension. I felt such love and I felt so much love from them.

3. I was in this amazing golden light, ... the warm light was "God" or my idea of God. I felt loved and cared for and precious, which was fabulous, and it seemed like everything made sense. "Ahhah" moment. ....this presence didn't tell me it was god - that was my later determination -

4. I just enjoyed the most wonderful peace and unconditional love. I think unconditional love doesn't do it justice, but I can't think of better words unless maybe "Awe Inspiring." ... I was like a baby wrapped in love. But the love was so intense, I did wonder a little about it I think. It felt new. Like a rebirth.

5. The feeling of love was enveloping all around me.

6. I felt the most immense sense of love and understanding. (Until this day this feeling has never left me.)

7. I then saw a bright gentle light coming down on me from the ceiling and it filled me with happiness and love that I never felt on earth. I

completely became addicted to it, it was so powerful. I let myself involved in it like I was bathing in pure euphoria. I never thought and cared anymore about my worries or fears about the errors I made in my entire lifetime.

8. [Did you see a light?] It was blinding, but out of it radiated the most wondrous feelings of love.

9. I heard a booming voice say, "I love you but you haven't experienced my gift to you yet. If you were to go now you would never get to see what it is like to..." and I woke up.

10. As I got further is when the overwhelming sense of my body absorbing all of this light it engulfed me. It washed me, it filled me up with such love I cannot explain. There is no word stronger than love here on earth to describe it.

11. I feel we are sent here to love one another in this big circle of life. Life to me is a big learning experience for all of us, almost like life is high school where you learn all you need to know and when you are finished you graduate to a higher realm which is heaven.

12. A feeling of Love so powerful and consuming, washed over me. It was so potent that you could almost reach out and touch it.

13. We are greeted by a "being" that is light, it's like a glow coming from it. I don't know if it's a she or a he. But it radiates so much love and safety it's indescribable.

14. I was blinded by the light unable to see anything but the light did not hurt your eyes. It was like looking into the sun a million times over

a pure white light. I felt warm, safe, peaceful, and in the presence of pure unconditional love.

15. All and any abuse or pain that I experienced in my life, whether it be physical, emotional, or mental, was completely gone and in its place, an intense love, acceptance, devotion, and sense of well-being was put.

16. It was totally dark & a soft light began to materialize. I suddenly felt the presence of intense comfort and love.

17. Profound feelings of joy and well being and happiness and comfort and love.

18. there was somebody with me and I felt safe and loved and at peace.

19. There was a light that defies description. It was so beautiful and seemed to be in complete harmony with sound and other sensory input that also defy description. It was not of this world. I felt content and loved, but this feeling was not separate from the light or sound or floating. Everything was all one experience. Nothing was separate from anything else.

20. I had a feeling of such absolute calm, love and peace which is simply not possible to describe.

21. I saw a light and I went into it. It was wondrous light that engulfed everything, there was total knowledge and love.

22. The greatest part was the full feeling and knowledge that in the end all there is is love.

23. Suddenly, all I saw was light. Not bright light, but soft, comforting light. I don't know how to explain it, like I said, it is too big for words:

Bigger than when you're in love, greater than when you hold your child for the first time.
24. An indescribable overwhelming love began to completely envelope me and with it came a sense of joy that defies words.

To be continued?

"NOT SUPPOSED TO": RULES AND ENFORCEMENT

1. We are not supposed to take our own life. I was fully aware of what I had done and the thought of being alone in that nothing forever was unbearable but what could I do? It was too late. Suddenly in the void I heard a voice, a male voice, and He said, "It's o.k. It's all right. It's all good."

2. When the person reached me we spoke through thought. He told me that it was not my time to enter into my heavenly home but had a mission to fulfill and my life was going to be very hard. I would go through many terrible experiences to the point of wanting to commit suicide, but if I committed suicide I would not be allowed to come home.

3. I was allowed to make the decision whether or not to return.

4. I wanted to go to the "sun" but someone telepathically told me I couldn't. I thought that I was awake and that my body was still in this world, so I stopped for a moment and wondered why the "sun" attracted me so, and why I couldn't go towards it. But at the same time I knew, I don't know how, that I wasn't allowed to go to the "sun." So I decided to disobey that voice inside of me that told me I couldn't because the attraction was really too great. Then in a fraction of a second, as I was attempting to go towards that light, I was projected into my body and I

heard some people who were telling me to throw up the water.

5. We get to this enormous light and I feel that my companion gets there before me, and I just know it's a boy my age: 17 years. We are greeted by a "being" that is light, it's like a glow coming from it. I don't know if it's a she or a he. But it radiates so much love and safety it's indescribable. The boy "disappears" into the light, but for some reason I'm not allowed to come along. I so much want to come too, it's so wonderfully comfortable. I feel so absolutely great. I stay by the light being, I can't get past it. I'm told it's not my time yet. Then everything goes black. When I woke up later I felt such an enormous sense of loss and disappointment because I couldn't go too. I'm almost angry about it.

6. [Did you have a sense of knowing special knowledge, universal order and/or purpose?] Yes, I feel that when death comes close, this one, death, allows you to choose whether you want to go or stay.

7. I remembered that I had a daughter, and before I could plead my case for returning, I was told by thought that I would not be allowed to stay. I got excited to return, and thought how much I wanted to remember the knowledge, so I could explain it to others, ease fears of death, and inspire goodness.

8. I was born a "totally awake" psychic. I saw and spoke with supposedly "dead people", including

the being known as Jesus, all of my life. I meditated regularly, and prayed regularly. I was accustomed to being out of my body frequently while doing this. I think this is why there was no "tunnel/white light" in my experience. I was already familiar with and comfortable on the "other side". Suddenly I was in a round Greek style temple that was not roofed. Jesus was before me and I was aware that there were 70 other people there to work with me. There was a mist that hid their faces from me, though I could see Jesus quite clearly. I was aware that each of them was working with me in my soul's growth and various karmic matters I had elected to work on during this body's sojourn. Jesus informed me that I had completed the work I had come in to do, and had "channeled" the 3 souls who would affect the future <my>. I could now stay with these beings, or I could take on another assignment and return to the earth plane. I don't usually make hasty decisions, and "he" knew that. I told him that was ridiculous. I would need time to consider the pros and cons of both scenarios, and that earthly body wasn't going to last for long. He laughed, snapped his fingers and my three children were standing before. I instantly knew that I had the "keys" that would unlock their memories when it was time for them to awaken, but that their father did not. If I opted to stay, they would have to come into the body again in another life to fulfill their destinies. I look at Jesus and said, "That's really unfair!! You know I can't leave them to come back again. This is emotional blackmail!" At which he cocked and eyebrow at me and laughed again. Then he responded, "But you do want them to succeed this time, don't you?" I replied, "Yes, you know I do. But I have a condition. If I go back, I want to be allowed to heal people. Not just their bodies, but their souls too. I want to awaken them to their soul's potential and Truth." Jesus smiled and answered, "As you desire, so shall it be." I awakened to my anesthesiologist cursing up a storm.

9. Then she saw IT, the music and colors that were indescribably beautiful and a light with such an intense beauty and mildness as never before. She was not allowed to go through.

10. The writing was like none I'd seen before. It reminded me a bit of Hebrew and runic writing. I couldn't read it. But I could read the mind of my guide! Hah! Blocked. ... I tried to memorize the shapes of the letters but was frustrated there as well. My guide informed me that I wasn't supposed to know what the entry said. I asked what was I allowed to know? I was informed that the entry described my life. It was hardly larger than a business card."That's all my life is?" I wanted to know. "Much more than that," I was told. "How so?" I asked. "People always do the best they can with the materials and information at hand. If an individual's resources are known, then the resulting choices can be anticipated." "So much for choice; everything is pre-

determined," I thought. "Not so," my guide said. "Almost all of your choices are free. It is the drive to do well which limits what you will choose. And it makes you predictable." "What, then, does the writing on the hide represent?," I asked. "A major choice which is not pre-determined by your resources." "What sort of choice is it?" "Knowledge of the choice would affect your decision." "Then I'd get it right, so tell me." "That would interfere with your free will." Round we went. Free will was something they would apparently bend Heaven and Earth to protect. The decision I was to make must be my own free choice. "Will I know it is the one, once I've made it?" "Perhaps."

11. I sense I was allowed to live for a specific reason. Although now a shut-in, I am in contact with people from all over the world via computer! I feel my purpose is to give joy and hope to those who are suffering

12. "Some were being welcomed with open arms and carefully guided through the transition point and into the wonderful light of the white tunnel; some were being greeted with discussions; and some were being turned back toward the earth plane."

13. Then five shadows began to form in the distance and come toward me, but they stopped. They were familiar to me, but I did not recognize them. When they stopped, I began receiving "thought talk". They were discussing whether I could go with them or not. Eventually I "heard"

that it "wasn't my time". I begged and pleaded in my own thought talk for them to take me with them, but they wouldn't. One shadow lingered behind and sent me a message that there was more for me to do. I woke up after two weeks in a coma.

14. The person took off his hood and revealed a man I call "Santa Claus." I was going to this island that he pointed at where people were happy and he told me about all the wonderful things there. It was the most wonderful experience. I was filled with so much happiness. Then I started crying. I told him that I did not want to go. I told him that I loved my husband very much, and I did not want to leave him. I also told him that I had a baby and I had other kids, I had to take care of that were just babies. I cried and cried, and begged and begged. He asked me over and over again, "Are you sure?" I told him, "Yes, yes, please, please, please let me go back." It seemed to take a very long time, but, he finally agreed. He told me that going back was going to hurt. He asked if I understood the pain that I would have going back. I told him I didn't care, I wanted to go back. He smiled and said, "Okay, you can go back, I will let you go."

17. I saw a figure of light come towards me out of the light. The figure told me "You must go back, we are not ready for you yet." I remember feeling like I did not want to leave. I kept saying, "Why?" "I don't want to go." But I was already leaving. I started to feel like I was falling from

the ceiling back into my body and I remember landing with such a big jolt that I woke up.

18. Then I heard a voice directly in my mind. I clearly perceived that it came to me from above-left side. This being I did not perceive as being "more" than myself. It was more like a "similar" to myself. A telepathic dialogue took place in which certain questions were asked and I was compelled to answer truthfully. At the end, I made a decision and at that point, the "void" stopped and, with difficulty, I made it back to the shore.

19. Everything was so crystal clear and seemed to make perfect sense although logically it was impossible. The figure told me "You must go back, we are not ready for you yet." I remember feeling like I did not want to leave. I kept saying, "Why?" "I don't want to go." But I was already leaving. I started to feel like I was falling from the ceiling back into my body and I remember landing with such a big jolt that I woke up.

20. I hear a voice saying "look up." I looked up, it was bright, and I look back down and back up, and I could see my soul leaving my body going in the air. Right then I began to pray to god to let me live because I wasn't ready. I just had a baby that May, and had three other small children. They needed me, and I needed them.

21. I was "sitting in God's lap," wrapped in the warmest embrace, and immediately involved in a "conversation." We communicated—telepathically? Don't know how else to describe

it. I didn't want to come back. That was my focus. I was Home, I liked being Home, just let me be Home. But God was holding me tighter (in the best of ways), and showing me the life to which I must return. ,,, God told me (crappy earth translation ahead) to stay true, "follow the clues," and all would be well.

22. Choking. I didn't feel any pain at all; however I was just struggling to set myself free from this man (the father of my son). I then was in this beautiful glowing place, white glowing background like clouds but illuminating bright clouds, and a man in front of me. A man in a white dressy shirt and white dressy pants, his hair so smooth black and short, beautifully comb to the back (very good looking man). I was begging him to let me stay, but he insisted in telling me I have to go back. I insisted in not coming back, I wanted to stay in this beautiful place. ... I knew I belonged there, however I tried hard, and implore, implore, and implore to stay in this beautiful world, forgetting and/or not caring to leave my two daughters and mother behind. I didn't care for leaving them; however I knew they were going to be alright. The feeling was so out of this planet, world or dimension. Again he insisted in telling me that I have to come back. It was like a little battle between this beautiful being and I.

23. I saw Heaven, a little to my left behind the pillars. It has Gold Wrought Iron Fencing with spikes on top. I saw the pearly gates. My three

angels, still perplexed as to how to get me back to my body, did not like my response of, "I don't want to go back down there; it is painful." "You Must! Your Mission is Not Yet Complete!" We communicated telepathically; no lips or mouth movements; all thoughts. My Three Angels sought permission from above to show me something. The clouds above their heads lit up as they cringed in fear, as did I. "Show Him!!" Was the response. The Angels flew me over to the right of these pillars - to what looked like a HUGE 4 Foot Thick Book, of LIFE. MY Life.

24. [Has your life changed specifically as a result of your experience?] Certainly I have more reverence for the privilege of life, and the love of my family and friends. But I am not sure what I am supposed to do with my life now.

26. I had chosen to come to this physical existence for a particular reason. I wasn't supposed to know what that reason was until it was time to fulfill my purpose.

27. [Note: There are many of these "not-your-time" episodes.] In front of me was something that's hard to describe, almost like an orb or a spirit of some kind. But I heard someone say, "You're not supposed to be here yet. Come with me and go back to your home, it's not your time."

28. [Note: There are many of these uncompleted-mission episodes.] The spirit, even though speaking in a soft female voice strongly repeated, "No! You have to go back." I again argued that I didn't want to go back. Then the

spirit on the right, in an even gentler tone said, "No Joe, you have to go back. There's something you have to do."

29. The only thing I understand about the second message is it is something I am supposed to share, because so many people don't understand the concept of physical life and non-physical life. ... I knew that people need to understand you don't see with eyes in heaven because eyes are part of the body and are necessary to see physically. When you are dead, you no longer have eyes to see with.

30. I heard a booming male voice loudly yell, "You are not supposed to remember this!" The next instant I found myself back in my bedroom.

31. "You don't belong here." I was sent away. I went to another place which was kind of a neutral place similar to this plane. I knew I was supposed to take a "class" or learn something. My experiential time was approximately a week although only a few hours had passed here. At this point I woke up from surgery.

32. My eyes felt like they were literally as big as saucers but I did not feel afraid, just very alone. The figures were in black, hooded cloaks similar to those of the ring wraiths in the Lord of the Rings. I did not feel like they were evil. One of them approached the other one and was floating. They did not appear to have feet or at least were not using them. There was no sound of any kind but I KNEW that they were discussing me and deciding what to do. I came back with the feeling

that I am supposed to be here. However, I didn't get the feeling of a great purpose or important work to accomplish, just a sense that things would not evolve the way they were supposed to if I didn't live out this life. I never felt as if I were being judged. It was more like they were reviewing the outcomes of sending me on or back. And you can see which one they chose (lol).

33. The writing was like none I'd seen before. It reminded me a bit of Hebrew and runic writing. I couldn't read it. But I could read the mind of my guide! Hah! Blocked. I tried to read it through one of the clerks. Frustrated again. I tried to memorize the shapes of the letters but was frustrated there as well. My guide informed me that I wasn't supposed to know what the entry said. I asked what was I allowed to know? I was informed that the entry described my life. It was hardly larger than a business card."That's all my life is?" I wanted to know. "Much more than that," I was told. "How so?" I asked. "People always do the best they can with the materials and information at hand. If an individual's resources are known, then the resulting choices can be anticipated." "So much for choice; everything is pre-determined," I thought. "Not so," my guide said. "Almost all of your choices are free." The writing was like none I'd seen before. It reminded me a bit of Hebrew and runic writing. I couldn't read it. But I could read the mind of my guide! Hah! Blocked. I tried to read it

through one of the clerks. Frustrated again. I tried to memorize the shapes of the letters but was frustrated there as well. My guide informed me that I wasn't supposed to know what the entry said. I asked what was I allowed to know? I was informed that the entry described my life. It was hardly larger than a business card."That's all my life is?" I wanted to know. "Much more than that," I was told. "How so?" I asked. "People always do the best they can with the materials and information at hand. If an individual's resources are known, then the resulting choices can be anticipated." "So much for choice; everything is pre-determined," I thought. "Not so," my guide said. "Almost all of your choices are free."It is the drive to do well which limits what you will choose. And it makes you predictable." "What, then, does the writing on the hide represent?," I asked. "A major choice which is not pre-determined by your resources." "What sort of choice is it?" "Knowledge of the choice would affect your decision." "Then I'd get it right, so tell me." "That would interfere with your free will." Round we went. Free will was something they would apparently bend Heaven and Earth to protect. The decision I was to make must be my own free choice. "Will I know it is the one, once I've made it?" "Perhaps." I noticed that this was nothing like I had been taught in Sunday School. I wondered if they really didn't know. Certainly, they had done nothing to prepare me for this experience. Then they got into a hushed discussion of what to do about me. I caught snippets of the conversation.- He has to reach a certain level of maturity in order to make the decision correctly. - If they put me into another body, it would be hard to get the right sort of parents. - Then, arranging the life experiences which would lead up to the decision would be very difficult to do in the remaining time. - How about putting him back where he came from? - His body is badly damaged. - Can we fix it? - Yes, but we'll have to change his life's affliction. - But, they cure that in his time! - Yes, but not before it has done its job. My next recollection was of feeling VERY sick. I thought I was still dying. Actually, I was beginning to recover. Ether can give one a truly vile hangover.

34. I had chosen to come to this physical existence for a particular reason. I wasn't supposed to know what that reason was until it was time to fulfill my purpose.

35. The figure told me "You must go back, we are not ready for you yet." I remember feeling like I did not want to leave. I kept saying, "Why?" "I don't want to go." But I was already leaving. I started to feel like I was falling from the ceiling back into my body and I remember landing with such a big jolt that I woke up.

36. I was going to this island that he pointed at where people were happy and he told me about all the wonderful things there. It was the most wonderful experience. I was filled with so much happiness. Then I started crying. I told him that I

did not want to go. I told him that I loved my husband very much, and I did not want to leave him. I also told him that I had a baby and I had other kids, I had to take care of that were just babies. I cried and cried, and begged and begged. He asked me over and over again, "Are you sure?" I told him, "Yes, yes, please, please, please let me go back." It seemed to take a very long time, but, he finally agreed. He told me that going back was going to hurt. He asked if I understood the pain that I would have going back. I told him I didn't care, I wanted to go back. He smiled and said okay, you can go back, I will let you go. We rowed back to the shore I had started on, and there was a man standing there. I could not see his face, but, he had black hair. He held out his hand, and I took it. We walked into a cave, or that is what it looked like. It was very dark. On the other side, was a huge light, a blinding light. I looked down, and I saw my body laying on a hospital bed. With a huge force behind me, I fell into the body that was mine.

37. It sounds funny because for them it was a life-threatening situation, but I was so calm and relaxing up there suspended in the air that I thought "This is death? How can I see if I have no eyes?" I then saw a bright gentle light coming down on me from the ceiling and it filled me with happiness and love that I never felt on earth. I completely became addicted to it, it was so powerful. I let myself involved in it like I was bathing in pure euphoria. I never thought and

cared anymore about my worries or fears about the errors I made in my entire lifetime. But then something was odd. I notice the medical team voices getting annoying and more loud and clearer they we're disturbing me keep saying, "Come on kid don't give up on me." I knew that my journey had ended. I needed to go in my body and I was not pleased about it.

38. At the same time, His voice was quiet, pondered and acute, but full of authority and love. I say authority because at the time when I wanted to speak, I felt that HIS VOICE PREVENTED me from doing so. He read my mind and answered the questions I had in my head.

39. I just recall being drawn towards a big bright light to the point where I was in the light, only to have it communicated (somehow) that it was time to leave and back I came.

40. Then the main lady talking to me said, "It's not your time yet you have to go back." Then she said, "Think about it, you remember," then it was clear at that moment, I said to her, "I'm dead aren't I?" She said, "Yes, but it's not your time yet, you have to go back. You are our go-between." I didn't want to and I proceeded to argue about it.

41. I felt that I was about to enter into Heaven. Just then, a lady's voice spoke to me, one of obvious authority. She said, "Don't go into the light. It is not your time yet." I remember bowing my head in disappointment. I awoke out of my coma.

INDESCRIBABLE PEACE

1. I started to feel a peace and well being which is indescribable.

2. My "pleasure" intensified to the highest degree the further I drew away from life.

3. I felt a peace and tranquility that I've never felt since.

4. I wasn't scared at that point. I was actually completely at peace.

5. It was the most wonderful experience. I was filled with so much happiness.

6. All around me I could see and feel a beautiful peace and tranquility with love and peace. I had no care in the world.

7. It felt like joy all around me. I felt fabulous, no pain, no worries, complete ment.

8. It was like having happiness running through your veins. [What emotions did you feel during the experience?] Happiness. Love, Joy. Every positive emotion you could drag out.

9. Everything seemed very calm, with no anxieties. It was a peacefulness which is very difficult to put into words.

10. I just enjoyed the most wonderful peace and unconditional love. I think unconditional love doesn't do it justice, but I can't think of better words, unless maybe, "Awe Inspiring." ... I was like a baby wrapped in love. But the love was so intense, I did wonder a little about it I think. It felt new. Like a rebirth.

11. It was the most wonderful, loving, peaceful feeling I have ever felt.

12. I felt wonderful and calm.

13. The feeling of love was enveloping all around me. There was no fear or sorrow whatsoever. ... It was pure joy and happiness. It felt more real than anything I've experienced on earth.

14. I then saw a bright gentle light coming down on me from the ceiling and it filled me with happiness and love that I never felt on earth. I became completely addicted to it, it was so powerful. I let myself be involved in it like I was bathing in pure euphoria. I never thought and cared anymore about my worries or fears about the errors I made in my entire lifetime.

15. The tranquility that was within there is now capturing my entire being, and was enough for this highly anxious girl to want to stay here for a long while.

16. I felt peaceful clarity. I was aware of the circumstances and knew I was dying. My face looked peaceful and oddly pretty. [What emotions did you feel during the experience?] Peace, absolute clarity, and an absence of pain.

17. [Did you see a light?] It was blinding, but out of it radiated the most wondrous feelings of love, peace and joy. I couldn't wait to join it.

18. I can't really describe the joy or calm I felt.

19. I felt wonderful—no body sensations; pain, density. Everything was light and pure, beyond anything describable.

20. I felt a very powerful all loving, , sensation

that I was Home! I was surrounded with a powerful energy source and was a source of positive energy myself.

22. It was the most welcoming and beautiful feeling I ever had. I felt so incredibly free and I was intensely happy and felt no need for anything. I just knew I never wanted to leave this sense of peace and wellbeing. One thing is for sure, I was NOT dead! I was more alive than I had ever been before.

23. I cried because I did not want to come back here because I felt so much peace and calmness and love that I never felt before.

24. I felt wonderful where I was. I floated very very peacefully through the air as I watched happily as I was being removed. During this time, I feel me riding as a little boy on a beautiful merry go round, lovely organ music, beautiful white clothes.

25. I felt calmer than at any time in my life. I have never felt so at peace or happy.

26. The draw toward the light was irresistible. I wanted to go. I kept walking toward it with an overwhelming peace and serenity. I knew I was dead. There was no sadness, no pain, no regret and no fear. All earthly thoughts were gone.

27. An extreme peace came over me. ... I felt complete peace, no worries about anything, and it was one of the greatest experiences of my life.

28. Then everything went black and I totally relaxed. It was a very, very peaceful, calm feeling. There was no pain, no stress, no worries.

29. The profoundly incredible peace was beyond conception.

30. I insisted in not coming back, I wanted to stay in this beautiful place. This Other Side, unexplainable in words. Too peaceful, too overwhelming, I was overpowered with so much love. I felt enamored, whole and complete, nothing to do with this world. It was my best experience in my whole life. The moment I step in the Other Side I felt the immense love all around me. ... I felt too much Joy, happiness, whole and complete. I felt perfect.

31. I awakened from coma with the feeling I had come back from the most beautiful journey you could do in a lifetime.

32. All I felt was a warm love, peace and a feeling of happiness that is difficult to put into words. ... For a long time I have longed for that feeling of love.

33. [What emotions did you feel during the experience?] I felt fantastic free release.

34. [What emotions did you feel during the experience?] A harmony that I never felt before or after the NDE.

35. This was the greatest feeling I had ever experienced.

36. [What emotions did you feel during the experience?] Total peace and calm. I have never felt such peace.

37. I felt so much love and beauty. It was a peaceful experience. I did not want to leave.

38. I felt this complete happiness and feeling of

just everything was lifted and I was to go.

39. At that moment, a great peace came over me.

40. I was floating above my own body and the sensation was euphoric. It was a feeling of perfection in the highest form. I was completely weightless, and hovering over my own body in complete bliss. ... The feeling was so good, so weightless, so careless and oblivious to any problems of the world, it was the most peaceful feeling I've ever experienced.41. Suddenly I entered a dark tunnel, feeling all the time at peace and in harmony, feeling wonderful.

42. All of a sudden I felt so peaceful the way I never felt before, a deep peace, the body no longer existed and it was as though it had never existed; none of my memories ever existed, pain never existed, memory of pain, no recollection of anything, only serenity and a white light all around me, blinding, a light cold in tone but warm.

43. The feeling I had was of infinite fulfillment. Then a moment came when I was brought up short by a "wall" of dense light, which gave off an unbelievable goodness, an indescribable love. ... This experience was so beautiful and I will carry it in my heart until I die.

44. I found myself encircled by an absolute warmness, in a state of satisfaction and light-heartedness.

45. I will never forget that face! It was so full of a welcoming, a non-demanding, warm smile of love. In that inviting face, as in the whole

experience, there was nothing else than a complete pure and total love, unlimited comprehension, kindness, and real affectionate, sympathetic and warm humour.

46. There was also no more fear, no more pain, I wasn't terrified anymore. It was peace, it was nirvana and I was happy to be there. I have never felt anything like it. I can still feel that feeling today.

47. [What emotions did you feel during the experience?] At first wonder, then an instant realization that this was death, then curiosity and an enormous "feeling of love." (I felt I was endlessly loved.)

48. I can not find the right words to describe very much after the tunnel. It was just so beautiful, feelings of peace and love and the "fullness of moisture" of everything (not the right words).

49. It all went black....just for a couple of seconds then this awesome light exploded in front of me and I stood in that light and I felt wonderful. It seemed to heal everything.

50. All and any abuse or pain that I experienced in my life, whether it be physical, emotional, or mental, was completely gone and in its place, an intense love, acceptance, devotion, and sense of well-being was put.

51. I suddenly felt the presence of intense comfort and love.

52. [Were there one or several parts of the experience especially meaningful or significant to you?] That feeling of peace was so strong. I am a

fairly highly strung person.

I only remember being drawn upwards in the tunnel, and that wonderful feeling of peace.

53. And at the apex of the tunnel, you are filled with a very bright light, a sensation of peace, a peace that is inexplicable to someone who has never felt it before. It isn't what people normally THINK peace is, but a far greater fullness of peace.

54. Profound feelings of joy and well-being and happiness and comfort and love.

55. I was calm and filled with utter and total peace. ... It was not of this world. I felt and loved, but this feeling was not separate from the light or sound or floating. Everything was all one experience.

56. I felt very safe and protected. I felt unconditional love, joy and profound peacefulness.

57. I had a feeling of such absolute calm, love, and peace which is simply not possible to describe.

58. I really didn't want to go back. It was so relaxing, restful and peaceful in the void.

59. [What emotions did you feel during the experience?] Peace—as if everything was fine and nothing bad or harmful could ever happen. With Peace came ment and happiness—not smiling, gleeful happiness but placid happiness and well being. And warmth, although warmth isn't an emotion, that is what I felt and remember.

60. Everything was so peaceful floating there. I

felt very safe and happy.

61. The experience was so beautiful and peaceful. I was also totally out of pain as the Light surrounded me.

62. I don't know how to explain it, like I said, it is too big for words: there was a peace coming over me. Rest, peace in it's greatest form. No worries, no problems, no bad feelings, no black thoughts. Only peace. Bigger than when you're in love, greater than when you hold your child for the first time, more beautiful than anyone can imagine. Only peace and rest and happiness. Nothing else.

63. I've never known such a wonderful and loving feeling. Nothing like here on earth. I so look forward to returning.

64. A beautiful feeling of a tranquil peace and wellbeing. ... An indescribable over- whelming love began to completely envelope me and with it came a sense of joy that defies words.

65. [What emotions did you feel during the experience?] A glorious warmth and relaxation.

66. I struggle looking forward to the day I can once again experience the euphoria of life after death. There is nothing like it and I want to search how to get it in this life.

67. There is NO PAIN...NO LOSS...NO PHYSICAL SENSES AT ALL. Only peace, calm, connectedness to the "all-that-is"...a true feeling of JOY...of "HOME". That's the only way I've ever been able to describe it.

68. I began to experience the most wonderful

sensation that I had ever felt. I was floating through what seemed to be a red tunnel of some sort. At the end of the tunnel was a bright light that did not bother my eyes at all. The light gave me a sense of strength and joy that is indescribable.

69. My first response was to wonder why my mother was crying because I felt very serene and peaceful.

70. I went towards this presence, which was within a brilliant, sunlight bright, light space - not a tunnel, but an area. The presence was unbelievable peace, love, acceptance, calm, and joy. The presence enveloped me and my joy was indescribable. As I write this I am brought back to this emotion and it delights me still. The feeling is spectacular.

71. I felt calmer than at any time in my life. I have never felt so at peace or happy.

72. It felt like a rocket-propelled orgasm. This feeling was like no other I had experienced, and like no other I have experienced since then.

73. [What emotions did you feel during the experience?] I felt a calmness and serenity I had never experienced before.

74. I felt a very powerful all loving, , sensation that I was Home! I was surrounded with a powerful energy source and was a source of positive energy myself.

75. I was not scared, I felt very peaceful. ... As I got further is when the overwhelming sense of my body absorbing all of this light it engulfed me.

It washed me, it filled me up with such love I cannot explain. There is no word stronger than love here on earth to describe it.

76. [What emotions did you feel during the experience?] Pure joy, clear mind, freedom, excitement, amazement.

77. I remember distinctly a humming noise like the sound of very powerful electrical current that was the most beautiful sound I have ever heard. It is so hard to explain but it is like a hummmmm, but as if it was played by the most perfect orchestra in the world.

78. I was at total peace and comfort. ... [What emotions did you feel during the experience?] Calm and relief from life.

79. I noticed a "light feeling" in the mid-sternum region. It felt really good so I allowed this "feeling" to continue. Within a few seconds I (?) was lifting, i.e., coming up out of my chest. It was the most incredible feeling of well being that I'd ever experienced. I kept saying over and over to myself, "I can't believe this feels so •••• good!"

80. A radiant being in long white robes was there to greet me. I could not discern the sex of the being, or the face of the being. However the most incredible feeling of love surrounded me. It emanated from the being. We were communicating through mental telepathy. I have never experienced such joy. All of a sudden I was back in bed with incredible pain.

81. The presence gave me the greatest feeling of unconditional love I have ever felt and sent me

back without ever speaking a word.

82. Next I traveled up through the light and now very clearly remember saying, "Wow this is great! This is better than any drugs that I took in college!"

83. A place of great "light". It is sooooooo-ooooooooooo beautiful. I feel so wonderful. I feel happy. I feel soooooooooooooooo much love. It is indescribable. There is so much love. The outstanding feature of this entire experience is the feeling (?), knowing (?), no, it's the love itself. A love I've never experienced on this earth. Never in my earthly life have I experienced the pure love. Not pure love. Maybe it was pure love. Or maybe it was "full" love of which we experience only minute aspects of it on earth.

84. Then a PEACE came over me. I felt like I was totally loved, totally happy. I had no fears or worries or pains. It was wonderful.

85. I felt fine...calm, not scared at all, just kind of interested in where I was.

86. I was very calm and relaxed with no thoughts whatsoever about events that were occurring elsewhere. No thought of anything in fact apart from feeling very peaceful.

87. After closing my eyes, the next recollection was myself being in the presence of, in the arena of, enveloped in, PURE UNCONDITIONAL LOVE. Re-reading this, it sounds so lame. How can I explain? For all these years I just have not been able to describe this to fully honour its incredibleness, it's ISNESS.

88. I now felt like I was warm and very loved and very happy to be there. I felt my sense of self begin to expand, like I was dissolving into the warmth of this reality, becoming a piece of a very wonderful whole. I wanted for nothing, except to feel like this forever.

89. I was two or three months old only when my heart stopped beating. All went calm, soft and dark and I felt more than fine. I felt at peace.

90. I felt wonderful, light, peaceful.

91. I felt MARVELOUS. Immeasurable joy inundated all my being. I felt no pain, no sorrows, nothing but wellness and delight as I had never experienced before.

92. Then it was as if I were floating backwards away from the room, into a tunnel of white illuminating warmth. It was nearly orgasmic it felt so good throughout my body.

93. One glance at this bright, splendid light made me feel safe, loved, and serene. I didn't feel pain or sadness, just an overwhelming peaceful love that grew more intense the closer I got to it. ... As I watched the light get closer and brighter, the sense of tranquil love grew stronger and stronger.

94. I saw a beautiful light. Very warm, inviting. I wanted to go to the light. I was warm. It was so bright, comforting, I was at peace and was drawn towards the light.

95. I felt surrounded/infused with this powerful "LOVE." It must be how a baby must feel whilst growing in its mother's womb. I don't know how

else to describe it. I felt safe.

96. There was no fear associated with this void, in fact I was unnaturally calm. Delightfully at peace (endorphins?)

97. I was being pulled into a white Light. I wanted to get there as quickly as possible, because all of these wonderful, ecstatic, feelings emanating from this Light: UNCONDITIONAL LOVE, FORGIVENESS, EMPATHY, COMPLETE ACCEPTANCE OF ME, DEEP UNDERSTANDING.

98. There was an extreme feeling of peace, words insufficient to describe the feeling.

99. It was one of the most beautiful experiences of my life and I will cherish it for as long as I live.

100. I remember feeling joy, not fear and being free from pain.

101. I felt this oh so strong love and a sense of everything being okay.

102. I felt a profound sense of peace and serenity than I have ever encountered. It was like I moved out from the tragedy to my inner self, a place that I found imperturbable, totally quiet and at rest.

103. The next experience is a profound feeling of calm and peace. I felt like someone had taken a black velvet blanket and wrapped me in it. The feeling was so comforting. I have never felt that kind of peace as strongly.

104. I lost consciousness. It was such a relaxed feeling, just slipping away like that. My whole being seemed to change. The first thing I noticed was an amazing sense of relaxation and calm. I noticed that every single negative human

emotion had simply gone, which left me feeling absolutely wonderful. Imagine the biggest high of your life, multiply it by a thousand, and you still won't even be close to this wonderful, safe feeling.

105. I was warm, loved, peaceful, and perfect, something I thought I knew until that night.

106. The feeling I experienced was so nice and peaceful, without a problem in the world. Everything was so perfect.

107. I get chills, tears, goose bumps when I relive this. As I tell it, my heart beats fast and I feel the incredible peace and love every time I share this, which is not often.

108. The peace was so overwhelming and so comforting.

109. The experience was peaceful and during the entire time I felt safe.

110. I was thinking it wasn't so bad. It was so dark but peaceful, and I remember thinking I must be dead.

111. The feeling of peace I felt was indescribable.

112. It was calm and peaceful.

113. The peace was absolutely overwhelming. I felt like I could burst at any moment because of the intense love that streamed through me.

114. I experienced such peace of mind and perfect love, unconditional love. I cannot describe it with mere words.

115. I remember feeling this incredible sense of peace and comfort, warmth and security. It was as if all my cares and responsibilities just melted

away. Prior to then and since then, I have not experienced anything so incredibly peaceful and seductive. It was extraordinarily beautiful to me, though I could not see anything.

116. I could hear an extremely pleasant and soothing natural chorus of insects and birds. I thought, "This is perfect. I want to stay here forever. I have never felt this wonderful!" I felt absolute clarity, peace, and love.

117. I remember the light up ahead. I had never known such peace.

118. At the time the feeling of euphoria was so intense that I was happy to go. I had absolutely no fear. I cannot describe the intensity of the calm, the peace and all the while being aware.

119. I knew I was dying. Everything was so peaceful with faint music.

120. It was the most wonderful feeling I've ever felt; there was total peace.

121. I was pure thought flowing in a wondrous river of peace and loving feeling.

122. I was totally peaceful; it was total bliss and total harmony at the same time.

123. Words could not describe the warmth, love, and peaceful feeling that was in this light.

124. Then, a complete calm and serenity overtook me. I was at total peace.

125. The environment was not hot, not cold. I felt a part of it. It was most pleasant and peaceful.

126. I really wanted to go into the peace and calm that had enveloped me, very much did I want to be a part of a higher energy form.

127. The peace was not to imagine.

128. I recall feeling peace. No fear and no pain, I was not happy nor was I sad.

129. The feeling was very peaceful. More peaceful than I had ever known.

130. There was the most wondrous peace, the deepest unity, and the greatest serenity anyone ever knew ... .

131. There was an immense feeling of love and peace that radiated from it and I never wanted to return to my previous state. I just wanted to stay in that light suspended for eternity.

132. I had a feeling of tremendous peace. Never had I felt peace like this before this time or since.

133. And I knew that Love and Peace and Joy and Truth and many other things are exactly the same thing and dwelt in the same place. And this was the place!

134. This was the most tranquil and peaceful moment in all my life.

135. I felt a deep peace and the most beautiful aesthetic feeling that is hard to describe at all.

136. He wore a simple white robe. Light seemed to emanate from Him and I felt He had great age and wisdom. He welcomed me with great Love, tranquility, Peace (indescribable), no words.

137. I felt a peace unlike any other, perhaps "The peace that passeth all understanding."

138. I become aware of how good I felt. I'd go so far as to say it was a feeling of peaceful bliss. That's an under-statement, but it's hard to describe the actual feeling.

EXTREMELY POWERFUL VISION

1. I became aware of my senses at that moment and how much more detailed everything seemed, and how it all appeared more focused and more sharp. It was like I was seeing the world for the first time with my own true eyes. It was the equivalent of taking off a pair of foggy ski-goggles or glasses.

2. I was alone in this place, or I thought I was at the time. I could still see and looked in all directions.

3. [Did your vision differ in any way from your normal, everyday vision?] Yes, did not feel like I was looking through eyes.

4. Suddenly found myself in the bedroom hovered over the bed looking at the clock and thinking, "Well when you are like this you can see perfectly without your glasses."

5. I thought, "This is Death? How can I see if I have no eyes?"

6. My realization was that I saw me from a new direction, and I watched myself for a few more moments.

7. The perspective of my memory at that point changed from looking up at him to looking down at the top and back of his head and myself from above.

8. My vision was extremely clear and intense–as if being in a body was like being in a lens, and

now it was clear.

9. I could see everything. Distance didn't matter. Everything was so much more real.

10. There is a super eye in our consciousness—I believe in this—the clarity of the vision is very much more powerful than the regular one.

11. There was no light. Everything was black and yet I could see clearly.

12. I had an altered type of vision because even though I was above the car I could "see" inside the car with a sort of "super vision."

13. As for the field of view, it encompasses all.

14. Although I was lying with my back towards the window, I was looking out of that window.

15. I seemed to be able to see my face although I was facing my back.

16. I could see farther, and almost a night-vision type look sight. I could see the trees perfectly clear. Even though my headlights weren't showing them, and there were no street lights.

17. Perception is different, you are not an observer, things happen within yourself, everything enters into you, vision comes towards you and it is something in a straight line, you are not aware of the sides, there is no lateral vision.

18. I seemed to have a spherical view 360 degrees vertically as horizontally.

19. I seem to think I was able to go vast distances very quickly to see what I needed to see or they wanted me to see.

20. My senses are two dimensional now, but not during this experience. The best way to describe

it would be that I could sense an added depth to things. This life seems flat compared to the other.

21. My peripheral vision was wider and I could see energy patterns around the trees as I passed, kind of like those optic fiber flowers you can buy.

22. [Did your vision differ in any way from your normal, everyday vision?] Do you know how big the letters on the label of a medicine bottle are? From the glass room I was in to the other end of the intensive care, it was about 15 meters (45 feet). Either I was standing next to them when a patient was administered medication, or I watched from my room.

23. While floating above the scene and seeing everything as if it were transparent.

24. I began to develop panoramic eyesight like a raptor.

25. [Did your vision differ in any way from your normal, everyday vision?] In the degree of my perception.

26. My vision was near 300 degrees. It was like being a short distance from my body, but I could also see what was happening behind me. ... My field of vision was enormous. I could see what was in front of me as well as part of what was behind me. Luminosity was very great.

27. I felt that I was able to zero in on any thing or anyone simply by drawing my attention to them regardless of the distance.

28. Normally I would wear glasses. During this experience, I could see clearly without them.

29. It was like watching High Definition TV, as

compared to normal: all people and things were vivid; there was no darkness or shadows.

30. One sense I recall was my sight zooming in closer. It was like it targeted right into the scene below with my body with a zoom in and out quality. As though just thinking about wanting a better view would "zoom" my sight in closer even though I was still on the ceiling level.

31. The first thing I noticed was my vision—the ability of my physical vision. From the mountain top I was standing on, the valley seemed to be MANY miles away, at least ten or so, maybe more. But I could see clearly every detail of both sides of the valley as I could the other. If one of the people were to have had a note in their hand, or two people had a note for instance, I would have been able to read them on both sides of the valley at one time. I don't remember seeing anything specifically, but I do remember how well I was able to see.

32. Although it was night, I could see everything, neighbor's houses, etc.

33. It "said," "In heaven (obvious god or Christian reference), what you need to understand is you do not need eyes to see." ... I knew that people need to understand you don't see with eyes in heaven because eyes are part of the body and are necessary to see physically. When you are dead, you no longer have eyes to see with.

34. I had lost my physical form and became a sphere where I could see all around me at once. It felt like a perfectly natural shape for me.

35. I had a general overview or a bird's-eye view. Plus I had the ability to focus quite closely on where I needed to (or where there was danger). It was as if my mind was a television camera with the ability to focus in at close range. Essentially, I had the sensation of experiencing the events from various perspectives.

36. You can see everything at the same time; there is no field of vision.

37. These images were all around me, 360 degrees of vision in a circle that curved up and away like a bowl. I watched as a section of the image became clear and bright.

38. I had the strangest thought that we are all floating around in a gas. Where we are going, there is no gas and everything is crystal clear, like diamonds. Here we are looking through a foggy gas, kind of like when it is very hot and you see those heat waves on a road as you drive.

39. I remember thinking, "Wait a minute, this isn't what it's supposed to be like." I knew my eyes were closed, but I could still see everything.

40. Now, here's something that is hard to explain. I was watching myself inside the tunnel at the same time I was looking at myself outside the tunnel. How could I be down in that tunnel seeing a light at the end of it when I'm floating out here seeing a tunnel that is not in a straight line?

41. I could see like there wasn't darkness just like a person can see when there is light in a room, but everything is black.

42. My eyes were not like earth eyes and I could

see different there.

43 It's as if I'm all eyes. I can see even behind me and darkness is all there is to see.

44. I could see clearly, even though it was dark and I was under the ice and moving downstream.

45 It was clearer than conscious life and much more profound.

46. My senses are two dimensional now, but not during this experience. The best way to describe it would be that I could sense an added depth to things. This life seems flat compared to the other.

47. I would say LIGHT AND EVEN SHADOW might (?) look like what nuclear physics can produce: light is made of small ultra bright dots, hyper mobiles and DENSE, energy. Colors are very, very vivid, clear, as if PURE, and each light dot that makes up the light seems to be individual, but it participates to the whole that constitutes the light, and it seems to contain the whole color prism.

48. [Did your vision differ in any way from your normal, everyday vision (in any aspect)?] It was as if I could see everything. There were no limits to what I could see if I chose to.

MIND-TO-MIND COMMUNICATION

1. They spoke to me with thought and I knew they were like me.

2. When the person reached me we spoke through thought.

3. They spoke to me, yet they had no mouths to speak, I just knew what they were saying.

4. A telepathic dialogue took place in which certain questions were asked and I was compelled to answer truthfully.

5. My guide spoke to me through my mind.

6. I didn't know all of them, they were greeting me telepathically.

7. The "being" spoke to me although the words were not heard with my ears. It was as if someone was speaking in my head, although it was not my voice I heard.

8. I remember knowing the purpose of life and why we are all here, as if someone was speaking to me.

9. Strangely though it seemed like I didn't need to hear words. I could just feel what they were saying.

10. The voice answered my thought with words of comfort, and peacefully suggested that it was not my time to go.

11. We communicated—telepathically? Don't know how else to describe it.

12. I remember bits and pieces of a "conversation" without words.

13. He read my mind and answered the questions I had in my head.

14. We communicated telepathically; no lips or mouth movements; all thoughts.

15. They talked to me through thought not sound.

16. I don't remember if I said that in words or by telepathy.

17. I was being spoken from within my own heart. It is hard to describe without sounding like I am making a conversation with myself, but that's what it was. It was like my inner conscience was talking to me. ... Again, the inner conscience 'spoke', and asked "Are you sure?"

18. We communicated mentally only.

19. I wanted to go to the "sun" but someone telepathically told me I couldn't.

20. There was a silent direct communication, which I am not able to "translate" into written or spoken words, neither specially into an image.

21. They communicated things to me in a way that I am not able to express them in words. How would I express something with two-dimensional communication tools that are four-dimensional?

21. Heard no voices but there was communication, knowledge and understanding.

22. My mother then looked at me and said, but not in words only in thought, "You have been given a second chance. I can take you the rest of the way, or you can go back."

23. This person was transparent but I could still see him smiling at me and saying to me, but not talking with his mouth but his mind, telling me,

"Everything is fine."

24. There was no hearing as such, more like telepathy.

25. Thoughts and ideas were being imparted to me as though people were talking to me.

26. They communicated with me with their minds, never spoke one word.

27. They were greeting me telepathically.

28. Something was communicating with me telepathically, and every thought was instant.

29. I think the communication was telepathic, we didn't talk in the usual way.

30. We were communicating through mental telepathy.

31. Communication was really different, as I didn't speak. I felt thoughts welling up inside of me and they were answered immediately. There were no words. It seemed that it was all feeling, all intuitive. Knowledge of anything I wanted to know was instantly transferred without language.

32. He communicated telepathically.

33. I remember hearing the prayers people would say in their heads as the Reverend prayed over me. I heard people's personal thoughts about me.

34. I'll mention that our talking was done by thinking. But, it wasn't intruding on one's thoughts. It was just the way we talked. We talked just by asking. But, it was all done without our mouths.

35. All communication was telepathic.

36. One figure approached me and asked politely, "What are you doing here?" Telepathy.

37. A communication occurred, through instantaneous osmosis, rather than our human verbalization.

38. The being pointed and no words but I could hear it speak, "Go now, you are not done."

39. We talked a lot, but I can't remember our mouths moving.

40. No one talked. It was like 'thought transfer' or something.

41. Something "spoke" to me but it was like the words were given straight to my conscience.

42. I remember saying, but not speaking, "I don't want to leave." I could hear the voice in my head saying, "Not now, your children need you, look up."

43. Although I don't believe that there was any verbal communication, there was perfect understanding.

44. I 'heard' in my mind that my father had died, but that I would see him again in a long time (when I was about 76). I argued with the voice that my father and mother had divorced. I was again told that my father was dead but that I would see him again.

45. A voice said to me: "Go back, it is not your time yet." This is also strange as it was not really a voice I heard, but more like a thought that was running through my brain (consciousness).

46. I would have been very willing to try to find a reasonable, scientific explanation for what was

happening until the staff realised I was actually reading their thoughts. They were all scared and I was also. At first I didn't know I was doing this. It seemed very natural and like real speech. I kept getting upset by their comments until they pointed out I shouldn't have heard them. ... At the time I was trying to dismiss it as a reaction to the anesthetic because I was terrified by what was happening, but one of the surgeons said, "That doesn't explain why you are reading my mind." ... I gave the doctor some details about his personal life that no one else knew. He was shocked and embarrassed. I picked words out of his head and said them back to him. He confirmed accuracy. I did this to all of the staff and asked them to say out loud if I was correct. This is when they started to look a bit nervous. I got them to acknowledge, out loud, that it's very unusual for a patient to wake up from the anesthetic with the ability to read minds.

47. It was as if we communicated in a form of a direct transfer of thoughts and ideas, a mind-to-mind kind of language.

48. Everything said was all telepathic as if energy thoughts coming across. Communication was fast. I didn't have to wait or think about it. I just knew. ... I realized how great communication is without words. Mouthing words is so slow.

49. We started to communicate telepathically.

50. We communicated without speaking, telepathically. ... People communicated with me without speaking.

51. I didn't hear a voice, but rather I was asked a question by this entity. It told me if I wanted to come out now I could, or I could go back. No voice, but I felt the question in a big way.

52. No words were spoken as it all happened telepathically. All I had to do was think about what I wanted to say.

53. While in my spirit body, I remember communicating telepathically.

54. Speaking to my mind he said, "You never die." I didn't understand and I asked him, "What do you mean I never die?" He said, "You never die," and soon I would understand everything.

55. We communicated telepathically.

56. I began receiving "thought talk."

57. The Being quickly asked me what the thought was that had just entered my consciousness.

58. A calming voice communicated into my mind the thought, "Yes, but it's okay."

59. These were not verbal conversations going on but rather a dialogue I sensed in my mind.

60. Our communication was different. It is not the same type of communication we have here. I was not talking. We could just send messages and understand each other (more telepathic in nature).

61. As I approached the light it spoke to me telepathically.

62. The main brightest light form addressed me mentally, saying, "It's not your time yet. You have to go back."

63. I then asked him why we were not speaking

the way we speak on earth and he told me that in the spirit world we communicated through our hearts and feelings so that there could never be any misunderstanding.

64. I received thoughts from other sources but I didn't see anyone.

65. There was no sound of any kind but I KNEW that they were discussing me and deciding what to do.

66. I did not hear anything audible from him, but basically telepathically he held out a choice for me.

67. Then, as if I were two people, a voice inside said "Hillari will be fine. Mama will raise her. She's good mother, and she did a wonderful job with me."

68. ... they 'said' (but it was not talking aloud) ... .

69. I suddenly remembered that this entity had "spoken" to me many times earlier in my life. I had always labeled the communication as "intuition." The "speaking" was clear, yet didn't really involve words (although I *remember* the conversation as words).

70. The [hospital] staff realised I was actually reading their thoughts. They were all scared and I was also. At first I didn't know I was doing this. It seemed very natural and like real speech. I kept getting upset by their comments until they pointed out I shouldn't have heard them staff.

REGAINED VAST KNOWLEDGE

1. It seemed like finally everything made sense. It was like an "Ah hah!" moment.

2. It was as if there was a force or energy out there way bigger than anything we know, and I had an enormous sense of understanding the meaning of life.

3. I remember knowing the purpose of life and why we are all here, as if someone was speaking to me.

4. [Did you have a sense of knowing special knowledge, universal order and/or purpose?] I had the impression I understood all in the universe, all the laws that regulate the universal life. All was obvious and simple, and all was connected.

5. So much "information." Personal, universal. Mostly about Thought and Love.

6. He [Jesus] said that there were many different religions on earth, as one faith would not take care of everyone's spiritual needs.

7. I felt enveloped in some kind of "knowing" that surpassed the human senses. ... The pain is left behind on earth. It does not travel with us, but the lessons we learn from it are eternal.

8. That you go to Hell after being a bad boy/girl is not a fact, it is just a political and religious concept to have you under control. Yes there is a purgatory, but it is not Hell with fire and torture. Not that you should do evil in this world, instead help one another. That is why we are here for, to

assist one another.

9. Our earth is Alive, as you are.

10. [Did you have a sense of knowing special knowledge, universal order and/or purpose?] Yes they told me that I had knowledge that I was to pass on.

11. I watched and listened suspended above my own body. At the same time it was as though all questions of the universe had been answered in that one moment.

12. At that moment everything appeared to be self-evident.

13. In this time I know all the energy into world, I know all.

14. I'm aware that for a while I "knew everything," but can't get hold of that knowledge again in my "waking" state. ... [Was the kind of experience difficult to express in words?] It's hard to describe feelings that are so strong, and the "knowledge" that all of a sudden you KNOW EVERYTHING.

15. I can't remember all of what it said, but if you asked a question in it it would answer you before you could think of it. But that knowledge was forgotten when I came back. ... Life is like school: be good to others, let others know life exists on other side...extend faith in God. And we are part of a bigger plan.

16. For one second...I understood it all, so simple, but then it was gone ...as if we are not meant to understand "ALL".

17. I was told everything that ever occurred and

everything that will occur. I was given reasons for what was, what is, and what will be.

18. I had spiritual guides who gave me what I call "a tour of the universe," and that was a sense of the vastness of the universe, of being there at its creation, of being a part of the universe from its beginnings, and I was part of all that has occurred, and all that will occur. It was like I had no sense of self, that I was everything and everything was me, including God.

19. When I told the nurse what she was studying for and how far she had progressed, she was incredulous. Afterwards she avoided me as if I were some sort of pariah. Another nurse I told of the medication patients were getting and she also reacted very strangely. After this, I did not mention it again.

20. I was then given a chance to view the universe and given the opportunity to be one with it and have the knowledge of the truth. This went into stuff like time is simultaneous, everything happens at the same time, there is no then and future. The universe is not just one but infinite, wondrous and continuing to evolve. We are just one dimension, there are many planes if you like. Just like ants are not aware of us, we are not aware of higher, evolved states of being. The greatest part was the full feeling and knowledge that in the end all there is is love. We become one with everything and everything becomes one with us. We are here to experience this life to the fullest and must be in the NOW to do that, get rid

of distractions, being addictions, destructive behaviors etc. We are here to be our best selves which includes being what we can for others. I no longer fear, in comparison I look forward to death. I was not wanting to come back.

21. I in a way had judged myself and clearly had an instant understanding of my life. And how important it is to play our lives out to the end regardless of how hard it is. And to get off of ourselves and to be in the company of each other to help each other.

22. Unnoticed by the people in the hospital, there were spirits or angels all around.

24. I continued on with a (person, spirit, being?) who was dressed in a monk gown. We went into the library where he proceeded to show me where the volumes of books were located that contained information on my various lives. He started to open a huge book called "The Book of Knowledge," when a higher up in the chain of beings came forth. He informed the individual with whom I was with, that I knew too much. And that he was to stop, and not open this book. The monk said that he wanted to show me where I came from, as well as three other members of my family. The picture was of a galaxy. And he did point out where we came from. All different locations in fact. The elder monk told him to stop at once.

25. I "learned" later that time and space only exist in the third dimension, and once one leaves it; there is none. There was no "here" or "there".

There was no definitive source of the light. The "space" just WAS light. ... It needs to be known to ALL...that on the "other" side...there is no HELL, or "bad" place. If there were, I definitely would have gone there.

26. I was told, but I didn't hear a voice, why everything was, and especially a lot about the earth which I cannot remember today. I just remember having this knowing of all things. And I looked at the earth smiled and said to myself, almost like a light bulb going off, "Oh! I get it." I understood and it was very beautiful.

27. For some reason everything seemed to all of a sudden make sense: the world, myself, everything was answered in an instant, and it seemed I knew everything.

28. I was pure intellect, absorbing information and knowledge through "sensors" or means that I have no concept of.

29. I asked how the universe was composed and it was explained to me in all details. I remember that it was extremely beautiful and extremely simple, and said to myself this information I must remember when I am sent back. ... I lost control over the information I got earlier. (It felt as if my head was crashed.)

30. The great difference is that after a NDE KNOWING has come in the place of BELIEVING/SUPPOSING/GUESSING. It sounds perhaps hypocritical, but I feel I am above all religions. I see religions as an attempt to create heaven or a connection with above, the creator

and the use of rites to make it easier to achieve that connection. Every religion and science is a restriction of the free mind. ... I can re-enter that tunnel at will and spend some time 'over there'. My wife notices my leaving my body as a uncontrolled shock, somewhat like in a seizure. I can acquire any knowledge and wisdom regarding humanity, society, science as well as individual people and use that in my own life. This knowledge may have to do with things that are about to happen, but I cannot change fate. I can only help people at that moment and after it happened because I am prepared and know the meaning of it. There usually is some 'key' to the use of that knowledge. It is understood that things are being developed and will come thru at the proper time via somebody's mind (invention, inspiration). A true enrichment is what I learned about former lives and the friends over there I can discuss essential life questions with. Of practical use is the service to anyone. I can ask questions for them and pass on the answers like a medium.

31. a) I began to "see" a progression of past lives. These were usually from the dual point of view of the person whose life I was viewing and from my own present perspective. b) I saw "runes"—some traditional, some unknown, in motion and in 3D and knew how they were to be interpreted. c) I had physical changes. For example, I had hot rushes up my spine and for two years had a 5-inch wide red itchy "stripe" up my back. I

virtually stopped sweating even in extreme heat, whereas before, I would break into drenching sweats when the temperature was in the high 70s. I slept much more than normal. When I was awake, it was difficult for me to stay out of an altered state. My libido increased dramatically. d) I found that my beliefs were forever altered. A skeptic, I was unable to remain so when I personally experienced many things that I had scoffed at. e) I found myself psychically "traveling"—more mental projections rather than out of body, although I have had a few of those. f) I got reams of channeled material, which was quite enlightening to me. g) My perception of energy movement increased dramatically, and I felt as if I could manipulate it. h) I went through a period where I seemed to be a conduit for unconditional love. This was somewhat disconcerting to me, as I, personally, felt no emotion, and yet people (strangers) flocked to me, smiled, gave me things, asked advice, and so on. i) I became a physical empath, i.e., I began to feel other people's physical pain and discomfort. This was uncannily accurate. The ability to do this extended to online and telephone encounters. The situation grew so marked that it caused me to avoid crowds, or even small gatherings. This situation continues to the present day, although it waxes and wanes.

32. There was a complete dialogue between myself and this unknown source. I "saw/understood" my life's purpose and how

easy it was to achieve.

33. I felt as if all the answers to all the questions I had ever had wanted answered, were answered simultaneously. It wasn't like I knew any one specific answer, more like I just knew everything there was to know, ever. I also had the feeling that as I received this knowledge from the beings of light, I in turn gave to them all the unique experiences that I had accumulated from my time alive on earth. They gave me what they had, and I gave them what I had to contribute. It was very pleasing to do this exchange.

34. I then found myself at the doorstep of a type of school, where there were a few students learning geometric shapes and physics with the accompanying healing energy involved. I thought the better way would be to go directly to the energy that is involved in the healing, direct from Source. ... I first sat in a healing chair to help my physical body heal on earth. Then we went to a vault that held information from souls' life cycles and growth. I was told I could have access to this information whenever I desired, it was important with the process of uncovering the dense dramas on earth. We also looked into a type of screen, that reminded me of a TV screen, and I saw a gathering of people in a field. They were all releasing the density that held back Unconditional Love, then holding the Light within and living within Peace above the dramas. After one man cleared himself out, another individual came up to him who was also cleared,

then they shook hands. Both bringing the Reality of Peace into their creative engagement, they both shared Light instead of any fear thoughts or actions. At this point, the Light streamed through them, all the density was then released into the Light. "It's gone! It's all gone!" I exclaimed! "I can see how this works, but who will believe me? I'm a nobody, my dad was a carpenter in Washington and I'll be a small town chiropractor. I think you should get somebody else! Besides that, I'm a bit shy!"

35. The only thing I understand about the second message is it is something I am supposed to share, because so many people don't understand the concept of physical life and non-physical life. ... Once people understand this concept, as simple as it is, then they will have the ability to be able to understand the concepts of the afterlife better and in the way they need to be thought of.

36. There were no more questions to be asked or problems to overcome. All is so simple. I just knew all the answers: there was nothing other than love and service... that was it.

37. They were asking each other if she knew. Knew what? I was a little unsettled then. What was I supposed to know? Where was I? ... Again they asked each other if I knew the answer. They were very busy trying to find an answer, maybe a formula, it was mathematical. They were looking inside of where I store my knowledge. I did not know it. A moment of feeling I needed to learn, and then a flood of information that I do not

remember.

38. In this state, I am aware they told me about my future and my purpose in this life, but in my dense human state, I cannot recall what I was told. I believe that everything has spirit— consciousness, if you will. All life, both seen and unseen, is energy. Energy is life—it all comes from the same Source. We are all One, everything is One, past, present and future. Time is only an illusion, made up to suit our earthly experience.

39. "All men have purpose." "You have purpose." "White man help the black man." "Organize."

40. There were several other revelations such as the origin of man, evolution, the meaning of the holy trinity, souls, my past life, etc., which were disclosed to me by a voice.

41. "As to what this is all about, you are in a physical body to learn to care about others, and to acquire knowledge. That is the sum totality of physical life."

42. I was held, and knowledge was imbued into me. ... There was also a tremendous feeling of love emanating from this source, and a kind of instant knowledge. You just knew it. ... I was given so much knowledge that it would overflow in your head normally, but I was told that each piece of knowledge would become available to me when needed.

43. Then I found myself in a blue tunnel. The colour was an electric blue, similar to the kind you get on certain L.E.D. Christmas lights now. It was a very vivid and wonderful colour. ... At this

point, the blue tunnel turned into the white tunnel, a very clear line of transition. ... The blue tunnel could accommodate two-way traffic, whereas the white tunnel was one way for souls leaving the earth plane. Once you crossed over into the white tunnel there was no going back. The light from this tunnel was so bright that under normal circumstances it would have been blinding, but here it was warm, safe and full of love. As I got closer to the transition point between the blue and white tunnels, the activity became clearer. I could clearly see many, many souls on both sides of the transition point. There were quite a few souls, like myself, coming from the earth plane. All of these souls were being met by groups of souls who had come from the white tunnel. It was like each soul had its own entourage of souls from the other side to meet them. Some were being welcomed with open arms and carefully guided through the transition point and into the wonderful light of the white tunnel; some were being greeted with discussions; and some were being turned back toward the earth plane. When I finally reached the transition, the first thing I did was carefully look around. This is how I gained my knowledge about the diameter of the tunnel. It was quite an amazing sight to behold, this transition point, with all the many souls coming and going. It was a very busy place, and most unexpected! When I was met by my own entourage of souls, I could clearly see that they were human, but in this existence were beings of light. They seemed to be the same colour as the electric blue in the first tunnel. I was greeted with a great love and urgency. I was held, and knowledge was imbued into me. I was told, this is not my time, but this was meant to happen.

44. It was impossible to see into the white tunnel, as there was so much light pouring out from it. There was also a tremendous feeling of love emanating from this source, and a kind of instant knowledge. You just knew it.

45. I know that all knowledge was in a structure with an enormous stairwell that went on forever up and to my left. ... I remembered what I had forgotten, which was everything. I was astonished at the simplicity of why, what, who, where...all of it. I knew it all. I remember thinking that it is so weird that we don't remember any of it on the other side. It's so apparent, yet we cannot see it while living in the other form. At that very moment I likened it to an ant that could never perceive a human in its entirety, it's complexity, or it's completeness, yet we are right there to be seen if only the ant had the capacity. ... I thought that maybe I could trick them; I would think of some words that perfectly described the knowledge in it's simplest form, and then remember the words. Then I'd associate the words and remember the knowledge. I came up with perfect words: all is everything, everything is one. I was so happy with my choice of words; I knew that I would remember.

46. I was looking into a star field—a massive, infinite entity that encompassed all of the galaxies, all of space, and some presence which is right in front of us all of the time that the earth sits in. It was massive and unimaginable. ... I realized it was seething with life, an ocean of blue and white froth waves being life and teeming with it.

47. I remember feeling very clear, having access to all my consciousness from the whole life and feeling the ability of pulling any thought or information if I needed to.

48. I went to a place of knowledge, where I knew everything. It was here that I knew that there was no such thing as time or space. It was here that I realised that I had created all of the melodramas in my life and it made me laugh. (I call that my cosmic giggle.)

49. Knowledge of many things on different levels simply appeared in my mind instantaneously. It's as if the knowledge of the ages all appeared in my mind at once. I was shown that our arguing and fighting are not what God intends for us. And, that we are meant to love and help one another. I felt deep shame at this. I've often wondered about the meaning of many things. I was allowed the answers although I wasn't allowed to bring this knowledge back with me. I retain the knowledge that it was shown to me. There is a reason for everything from the smallest drop of rain to every last grain of sand in the deserts. I was shown the reason for everything in the

matter of a couple of seconds. I'm not surprised that I didn't retain the knowledge. To say that man simply cannot comprehend the greatest of God is more than an understatement.

50. I felt the depth and breath of eternal knowledge and the wisdom of the ages within me.

51. I remember learning that all spirituality is good. Not one belief system was better than the other.

52. They told me I would not have children, but I would come to be at peace with it. I always knew I could not have children. I had a hysterectomy without ever having children. Our dogs and cats are like our children. ... I saw myself starting to become successful and I had glasses. I would get glasses, which I got at the age of 25. They told me that I would have someone very special, a true love to love me the rest of my life. I always knew that I would find that some one. ... They also told me I would be very successful in life professionally and do great things for others. I am now starting to do many things in my profession.

53. It was like I was carrying with me the essence of everything I had lived through during my life. But most important I had TWO kinds of experiences with me. Those that made me feel happy and satisfied and those that made me feel sad and disappointed.

54. It was an experience where everything was instantly self-evident. If I turned my awareness

to anything, it was self-evident to me with no time delay. I experienced that I was free in time and space; they were not obstacles to my awareness. I KNEW what I was experiencing. It was clear.

55. I also experienced extreme clarity of why I had the cancer, why I had come into this life in the first place, what role everyone in my family played in my life in the grand scheme of things, and generally how life works. The clarity and understanding I obtained in this state is almost indescribable. Words seem to limit the experience - I was at a place where I understood how much more there is than what we are able to conceive in our three-dimensional world. ... I realized what a gift life is and that I was surrounded by loving spiritual beings who were always around me even when I did not know it. ... I was shown how illnesses start on an energetic level before they become physical. I then understood that when people have medical treatments for illnesses, it rids the illness only from their body but not from their energy so the illness returns. I was given the understanding that this applies to anything, not only illnesses - physical conditions, psychological conditions, etc. I was shown that everything going on in our lives was dependant on this energy around us, created by us. Nothing was solid. We created our surroundings, our conditions, etc., depending on this energy. The clarity I received around how we get what we do was phenomenal! It's all about

where we are energetically. I was made to feel that I was going to see proof of this first hand if I returned back to my body.

56. There was no past, present or future. Only everything all at once. I felt a tremendous understanding of the nature of the universe and my place in it.

57. He showed me what looked like a huge white obelisk floating in the blackness. As I looked at it more closely, I saw that the surface was moving. It was a giant puzzle and it looked like it was being solved. He showed me my place and how the puzzle was re-arranged with each action by anyone on earth. Some of the puzzle had already fallen into place and I knew that something wonderful was going to happen when it was complete. Of course, I don't remember what it is but I still look forward to it!

58. I was presented with a sense that all questions were to be answered if I stayed.

59. The universal wisdom I gained in the light vanished when the light left.

60. I was in another land. ... I met people and we just knew everything.

61. There's someone there with me, a presence I can only feel. Suddenly I know and understand everything. I know what everything is like, and I know I'm in the realm of death.

62. I was asking questions but knew the answers instantly. Heard no voices but there was communication, knowledge and understanding

HOME

1. I would go through many terrible experiences to the point of wanting to commit suicide, but if I committed suicide I would not be allowed to come home.

2. My life did "flash" before me; however this "review" did not stop at my birth. My recollection was going back in time and "space" well before my birth.

3. He told me that it was not my time to enter into my heavenly home.

4. I saw people on this seashore, and I seemed to know these people even though I have never seen them in this dimension. I felt such love and I felt so much love from them.

5. I was just in another place, somewhere I'd always been. These people knew me and I knew them. I had no memory at all of any previous life. It was more real to me than anything else I'd ever experienced, but the most important thing was, that these people were so lovely. Kind, funny, loving, considerate. It was like having happiness running through your veins. [Did you meet or see any other beings?] I knew them, but none of them were people from my life here. They were just people. It was just life, only better.

6. I can't really describe the joy or calm I felt. I wanted to go so badly. It felt like home.

7. I felt a very powerful all loving, , sensation that I was Home! I was surrounded with a powerful

energy source and was a source of positive energy myself.

8. Since then I feel sort of Homesick and a sense of not belonging to this world. For I know this is not my home.

9. There was no sadness, no pain, no regret and no fear. All earthly thoughts were gone. I was going home.

10. I didn't want to come back. That was my focus. I was Home. I liked being Home. Just let me be Home.

11. [What emotions did you feel during the experience?] I knew I belonged there. It was a feeling I been there before, but I can't point a finger of when.

12. It asked, "Are you ready to come home?" I knew it meant death.

13. Nearly as if I had been away in a long, long journey in a foreign country, and after a time I finally had come back again! Home, where everything was so well-known and safe.

14. Flat lined. Went to a place that was beautifully lit, like the sunshine, but much prettier and more golden (kind of like sepia tones). Seemed like a neighborhood, and I was shown around to all the people I loved and missed and they were all so happy. I remember being surprised like: "Oh! Hi....wow you're here, how nice," and smiling very broadly. I remember my Dad sitting on a stoop of sorts with his hand outstretched to me. He was many years younger than he was when he died, and I was just a

toddler reaching up to him. I know I saw lots of people, but can't remember who they were specifically, except for my Dad.

15. My personal feeling is that we are all "sparks" that come from the "Big Light." When our physical bodies die, our soul, spirit, essence, feelings and thoughts, go back to the source....the "LIGHT."

16. A voice said to me: "Richard, why are you here?" I said, "I want to come home." The voice replied: "It's not time yet. You have more work to do." ... I felt I was home where I belonged. I was incredibly sad when I had to leave.

17. He didn't say a word but I heard, "It's OK we are going home."

18. Only peace, calm, connectedness to the "all-that-is"...a true feeling of JOY...of "HOME."

19. I felt a very powerful all loving, , sensation that I was Home! I was surrounded with a powerful energy source and was a source of positive energy myself.

20. I was still communicating my desire to stay home (for I felt I was home).

21. I was home. At last I was at the place I had been looking for for so long. ... I now KNOW we can ALL go home.

22. I just slid out of my body and rose above the bed and said to myself, "I thought this one was supposed to be longer. Oh well, I am coming home."

23. I saw many beings of light waiting for me and saying, "Welcome back." They were happy to see

me again and they were welcoming and radiating all their love to me. ... We belong there...for it is our home.

24. Death is not the end, only a transition to our true home.

25. I would look down and see a white stone path with people waving; I had a feeling that I knew them. It's like they were waving hello.

26. I felt the most overwhelming sense of belonging, like I had come home. ... I was aware that behind me were other energy beings, people who I knew so well, like I had really come home.

27. I said, "Lord will I go home now?" He answered, "No, it is not your time. Your mission is not complete. You have to return."

28. Even though I love life and am so thankful for each and every day, part of me wants to be "back home."

29. "What are you doing here?" he asked. "I belong here," I replied. "That I know, but what are you doing here NOW?"

30. I was filled with bliss and comfort, and felt "at home" for the first time ever.

31. I was home. I felt total love from this presence. I was home. More so than I was ever home before.

32. There was something familiar about this "place," as if I had been there before, but more like I had returned to whence I came.

33. I felt like I was "home." This was where I had come from, this was where I belonged.

34. It then occurred to me that I must be dead.

Then I did the "Home again, home again! boogie." It was sublime.

35. I gave no thought to my beloved pets, family, friends, or plans. I was so excited to go home.

36. I was with my biological mother who passed 12 yrs earlier and countless others who loved me and were so happy to see me and I them.

37. My angel and I were like flying toward this really bright light. The light was getting closer and then and in a second it just engulfed us. It was thousands of times brighter than the sun and yet my eyes did not hurt. Somehow I knew I was home.

38. I was in another land. The most wonderful and beautiful place I have ever seen. ... I met people and we just knew everything.

39. It was like my inner conscience was talking to me. It asked, "Are you ready to come home?" I knew it meant death.

MISSION TO ACCOMPLISH IN LIFE

1. I was told it was not my time and that I should return to finish my life's work. There was no negativity about it but a comforting gesture to return, that I was there by accident.

2. He told me that it was not my time to enter into my heavenly home but had a mission to fulfill and my life was going to be very hard. I would go through many terrible experiences to the point of wanting to commit suicide, but if I committed suicide I would not be allowed to come home. He told me that I would be watched over and protected, kept safe. If I would get through this mission I would be allowed to return home.

3. "I don't want to go back down there; it is painful." "You must! Your mission is not yet complete!"

4. [Did you have a sense of knowing special knowledge, universal order and/or purpose?] Yes they told me that I had knowledge that I was to pass on.

5. I started arguing with God in my own little obnoxious way, and God said I needed to go back because my mission here wasn't complete.

6. I felt a very strong feeling of depression or failure or something along those lines. This persisted throughout the experience. This is just an interpretation based on subsequent studies of NDEs, but I think it probably had to do with the

way I got there (suicide attempt) and the fact that I hadn't completed my mission.

7. A voice said to me: "Richard, why are you here?" I said: "I want to come home." The voice replied: "It's not time yet. You have more work to do. You have a family that loves you and that you need to take care of."

8. I also felt that I had a purpose, a mission that was not yet fulfilled in this life. This was not a work I had to finish, but rather a stage that I had to complete in this life, a form of spiritual growth.

9. The next memory I have was standing again outside the light in the delivery room and saying, "I choose to live," which I presume was a decision to come back on earth for my mission was unfinished.

10. [Is there anything else you would like to add concerning the experience?] I wish I had been older at the time of this event. It has helped me to accept the real presence of Our Lord and know that He is all powerful and that my life is in His hands. I feel that He still has a job for me to do before I depart this earth. Now that I have raised my family, I am ready to go to the task.

11. His parting thoughts, they came to me, and have always been a mystery, "Your life's not done, you've a purpose still, a mission you're on, you've yet to fill."

12. I heard a voice tell me, I could "not remain" there, I would "have to go back." I asked, "Why not?" and was told that I would "have to finish

what I had started out to accomplish."

13. I did not want to re-enter my blue body that I had seen lying down there on the white tiles. Then I got a message 'from above' to return and do what was in stock for me.

14. I "saw/understood" my life's purpose and how easy it was to achieve. I was asked whether I wanted to "go back and continue what I had started" and I emphatically said, "Of course."

15. A communication occurred, through instantaneous osmosis, rather than our human verbalization. The communication concerned my pre-natal chosen human life's work as well as some basic universal laws, which I had overlooked in my human form. Then it was time for me to return. I did not want to return to my human form.

16. I again argued that I didn't want to go back. Then the spirit on the right, in an even gentler tone said, "No Joe, you have to go back. There's something you have to do.

17. I am aware they told me about my future and my purpose in this life, but in my dense human state, I cannot recall what I was told.

18. We reviewed my life and also discussed my mission in life.

19. I felt something inside of me, like I did not accomplish a task. I did not remember what it was, but I knew that I had to do it. I remember saying that I have to go back.

20. I told my angel that I wanted to go back to earth. He just smiled and told me that my mission

was not done. (I still don't know what my mission is.)

21. I asked, "Lord will I go home now?" He answered, "No, it is not your time. Your mission is not complete. You have to return."

22. When I hit the rock for the final time, my spirit popped back into my body. Since this experience I have a better understanding of life and my personal purpose.

23. I had heard this wonderful, familiar voice, "It is not yet your time to be here. You must go back." I begged it to please not send me back. And that is when it told me I had a mission to do. I begged it to please tell me the mission so I could do it and come back. Then it told me I had to go back and perform my mission when the time came. I would not know what it was until that time.

24. ... from this perspective I knew my powerful nature and saw the amazing possibilities we as humans are capable of achieving during a physical life. I found out that my purpose now would be to live heaven on earth using this new understanding and also to share this knowledge with other people. ... Then I saw how my husband's purpose was linked to mine and how we had decided to come and experience this life together. If I died, he would probably follow soon after.

25. I came back with the feeling that I am supposed to be here. However, I didn't get the feeling of a great purpose or important work to

accomplish, just a sense that things would not evolve the way they were supposed to if I didn't live out this life.

26. A voice said to me: "Richard, why are you here?" I said: "I want to come home." The voice replied: "It's not time yet. You have more work to do.

27. The entity then "reminded" me that I had not fulfilled my purpose yet. Suddenly, I remembered events that had happened before I was conceived. I had chosen to come to this physical existence for a particular reason. I wasn't supposed to know what that reason was until it was time to fulfill my purpose. I also knew that I could stay in this other place without fulfilling the purpose and it wouldn't be held against me. However, I felt it was better to go back ("to" Earth), fulfill my purpose, and then return.

28. Suddenly, I remembered events that had happened before I was conceived. I had chosen to come to this physical existence for a particular reason. I wasn't supposed to know what that reason was until it was time to fulfill my purpose. I also knew that I could stay in this other place without fulfilling the purpose and it wouldn't be held against me. However, I felt it was better to go back ("to" Earth), fulfill my purpose, and then return.

29. After gazing in the Book he looked down on me and said, "You must go back, it's not your time." I remember the wonderfully beautiful feeling overcoming me and thought, "I don't want

to go back." He must have heard my thoughts because he said to me, "You have something to do before you can come here." I asked, "What must I do?" as he said nothing and closed the Book. As soon as the Book closed I awoke in my body.

30. [What was the best and worst part of your experience?] Realizing we all have a purpose in life and what we do with it is up to us.

31. And also saw my future that I had not experienced having children yet, and had a lot more things to accomplish. It was not my time.

GUIDES

1. Suddenly I found myself in darkness where something or someone was drawing me to them, and the closer I got the more comfortable I felt.

2. Through all of this I felt someone next to me. I think it was a woman because it had woman's voice, but she did not speak with her mouth. This woman (?) showed me things. I do not remember all. She said to me, "This is what it will be like when you come here." ... I felt her next to me at all times. She was so calm.

3. I was accompanied by someone. I suppose it would have been a woman, because she had a brown skirt on. ... The "person" at my side guided me in the other direction.

4. [Did you meet or see any other beings?] An outline of a human form. It brought me back. I was not aware it was of a human form when I was in its presence.

5. I felt the presence of someone beside me, on my left. I knew he was there and without having to look I knew exactly what he looked like. He was dressed in a colourful something or other but what stayed with me was his face. He had long shoulders, brownish-fair slightly curly hair, a longish face darkened by a short beard and the most amazing eyes. They had a colour between pale blue and light grey. Although I knew he was there I never turned toward him. I was intent on going into the light but as I was moving toward it

Iheard him. "What are you doing here?" he asked. "I belong here", I replied. "That I know but what are you doing here now?" he asked again. A thousand answers were ready to come out of my mouth, but before I had time to voice them I knew he was right so I kept my silence and waited. "It is not your time yet" he said in a kind but also firm way. "You still have a lot of work to do." I wasn't ready to give up yet. I was readying myself to refuse, but then something inside me realised the truth of what he had said. And that was the moment I opened my eyes and saw my sister standing above me.

6. I recall clear as if it had happened yesterday, sitting up out of my body and looking at a man who was sitting on the chair close to where my body was. I recall laughing as if I was incredibly happy to see him. I felt like I had known him my entire life. He was sitting down, he had blondish brown hair and was wearing a white shirt with blue jeans. He had his face covered so I couldn't see it and he was shaking his head from side to side as if he was disappointed in me. The next thing I remember was opening my eyes to see the paramedics and my mom standing over me.

7. Finally, the end of the tunnel is here, and I am enveloped in that same light, that without a word spoken, directed me here. Within a few seconds, a lady appeared, to tell me that I had a choice, and that I was young. Looking at her was my new agenda. Who is she? I don't recognize her, but she seems to know me. I continue to do a checklist of

her characteristics. She has shoulder length, strawberry reddish hair, and very pale skin. Her eyes were a stunning blue. At this point, it did not matter where I knew her from, or who she is. I had a choice to make, and she made me feel that time was of the essence. I wanted to stay, but had remembered her saying that I was young. What did that mean? Does that really have anything to do with my choice? She was about 50 years old, and looked extremely happy! What a decision to make. This is the best vacation ever! I needed more time, but she gave an insistent order to make my choice and said whatever I choose will be fine. At that time, I turned around, back to the direction I had so calmly came from, and was immediately pulled back through the dark tunnel.

8. ... I was greeted with the most handsome spirit who guided me through this experience.

9. [Did you meet or see any other beings?] Some power was also traveling along with me, beside, I felt. I don't know whom it was.

10. A being of white light appeared to me and took my hand and took me to a door that opened on its own.

11. I was thinking about these feelings when I felt something "move" near me. ... I recognized the "movement" as being the movement of an entity. I "recognized" that this entity had been with me all my life. I don't know if it was what people call a guardian angel or if it was just another disassociated aspect of my psyche. However, I

suddenly remembered that this entity had "spoken" to me many times earlier in my life. I had always labeled the communication as "intuition." The "speaking" was clear, yet didn't really involve words (although I *remember* the conversation as words).

12. Then I saw a tunnel that was lit up with white light but it wasn't hard on the eyes. Then I noticed I was following another being whom I didn't know toward the tunnel for a long period of time. I couldn't catch up to this person. This peaceful state lasted for some time but then I felt intense pain and burning in the chest again. Apparently the paramedics zapped me. ... I did talk to a Shaman from the Ojibwa Tribe in Northern Wisconsin and he told me the figure I was following toward the tunnel was my spiritual guide. To this day I believe him.

13. I hear a voice saying "look up." I looked up, it was bright, and I look back down and back up, and I could see my soul leaving my body going in the air.

14. At one point I became aware of a light that was with me that I'll refer to as a presence. The presence was communicating with me, and assuring me I was safe, and led me through a beautiful field with flowers and trees and a creek. The presence was telling me I would no longer have any worries or troubles, and was so calming. We got to a white bridge and I was ready to go over when the presence said it was

okay to go over but told me I had three small children on this side, so I remained on this side.

15. There was someone on my right holding my arm taking me. I could tell that this person KNEW where we were going and it was their mission to bring me. I was screaming no, no, no. I did not want to go. I could see objects going by me on each side. I don't know what they were because we were flying so fast. It felt like we were going down that dark hallway for a long time. I remember just thinking "No. Where am I?" Where are we going? Then we stopped in front of a door on the left. I don't know what color the door was, all I knew was it was a door and I was not going through it! I kept saying NO! The next thing I remember was my husband telling me I had a seizure.

16. Anyway, to my right was someone very awesome, a male. This big love seemed related to this being. I didn't know who it was but I was very awestruck.

17. I was aware of a presence that was at once familiar and loving and kind and all powerful and so very immense that there will never be any words appropriate to describe this thing. ... Suddenly I was given a choice. I could go back to earth and back to the human body that I was living in, or I could stay in these realms. ... That was the last thing I remember before coming to in the hospital.

18. The most incredible of all was this woman came to me and held my hand and stayed with

me the entire time until the paramedics started to treat me.

19. I felt something or someone was there, it seemed I was given a choice to stay or go back.

20. I hear a voice. Not with my ears, but in my head, I couldn't see a source, but I knew exactly what point space the voice was coming from and I knew, it was directed at me. In fact that point in space was watching me closely. I couldn't see it with my eyes, or hear it with my ears, I just knew. And it all made perfect sense. This voice then invited me to walk forward. It said that if I took on step forward I would be able to feel that way indefinitely. It seemed like the right thing to do. I didn't even think about it, I just lifted my foot and started to step. Then the source of the voice looked away from me, at a dark haired female. I had not seen her before. I don't even remember if I saw her with my eyes or only in my mind. All I really remember is that the voice was now looking at her and she had very dark hair. The voice then instructed her to go back, that she wasn't ready yet, and I stopped. I told the voice that I wanted to go back with the female, and to help her. That I wanted to feel pain again, that I wanted to feel alive, and to laugh, and to cry, and to hurt if I had to. ... I was ripped back into my body.

21. A voice came. A male voice just kind of matter-of-factly said "you are drowning."

22. A light appeared and there was someone, an entity, in two dimensions, without human

features. I noticed other presences, as if they were accompanying me, but there was no one I knew. [Did you meet or see any other beings?] I saw a presence but did not know it, then I felt other presences but did not see them. I felt that they were behind the first being, and they told me I had to go back, as I still had things to do, that my moment had still not come.

23. There was someone close by, I can't say who it was. And I was fascinated by the "sun" that I saw shining overhead. It drew me towards it, it was irresistible. I wanted to go to the "sun" but someone telepathically told me I couldn't. [Did you meet or see any other beings?] There was someone to my right but I don't know who. I didn't look at him.

24. He said his name was Michael and for me to come with him. I looked and there was a tunnel where he was.

25. [Did you meet or see any other beings?] I'm not sure, seems as if there was somebody in the big room with me.

26. The only thing I remember is that I saw a pathway of stones, and I walked along it with someone who took me by my hand. We went towards a resplendent light. I wasn't afraid at any time. I didn't see the face of the person I was walking with, nevertheless he wore a white tunic and I walked on his left.

27. There's someone there with me, a presence I can only feel. We are greeted by a "being" that is light, it's like a glow coming from it, I don't know

if it's a she or a he. But it radiates so much love and safety it's indescribable. ... I stay by the light being, I can't get past it. I'm told it's not my time yet. Then everything goes black. When I woke up later I felt such an enormous sense of loss and disappointment because I couldn't go too, I'm almost angry about it.

28. At this time I was being pulled at a high rate of speed and there was somebody with me and I felt safe and loved and at peace. This person was transparent but I could still see him smiling at me, and saying to me, but not talking with his mouth but his mind, telling me, "everything is fine."

29. I turned around in some sort of concrete swimming pool, and I was not alone there. Somebody else turned around with me. ... All of a sudden somebody appeared in front of me. He was young with a beard. I told him, "When do I go back down to earth???" and he said, "But you are already on earth." I did not believe him and I asked the same question again, he replied the same answer, and I got back down into my body ... .

30. Air brushed behind my neck as though someone was behind me. Then all of a sudden I heard a voice coming toward me. A man's voice which was in a different language. It was more of a whisper that turned into English, telling me "It's almost time." I saw quick pictures of myself aging from childhood to adulthood and more forward. All of a sudden a jerk came across my

body and it automatically shifted 180 degrees. I then opened my eyes laying in a hospital bed wondering what the heck had just happened.

31. ... I knew the woman was beside me. I did not really see her, but I knew she was there. It was so beautiful. I cried from happiness. From one to the other, I felt like someone or something was pulling me away. The landscape faded and I was back on the operation table.

32. A spirit guide told me to breathe deeply. A sweet perfume scent filled the air, which made it easier to relax and let go. We went through a powder blue-white light. I was shown a glimpse of my future. I continued on to a library of sorts. (I've since been to this library three times). There were small groups of people or spirits (?) in individual rooms called "pods." In these rooms the spirits or people, were planning their next life or reincarnation. I continued on with a (person, spirit, being?) who was dressed in a monk gown. We went into the library where he proceeded to show me where the volumes of books were located that contained information on my various lives. He started to open a huge book called "The Book of Knowledge," when a higher up in the chain of beings came forth. He informed the individual I was with that I knew too much. And that he was to stop, and not open this book. The monk said that he wanted to show me where I came from, as well as three other members of my family. The picture was of a galaxy. And, he did point out were we came from. All different

locations in fact. The elder monk told him to stop at once.

33. Then I gradually became aware that I wasn't alone, and I'm not talking about the other people in the ward. There was an unseen 'someone' approaching me. An indescribable overwhelming love began to completely envelope me, and with it came a sense of joy that defies words.

34. When I died, I rose above my body and saw my grandfather working on my body. My body was of no interest to me; instead I moved out of the room towards a presence I felt in the living room area. I went towards this presence, which was within a brilliant, sunlight bright, light space—not a tunnel, but an area. The presence was unbelievable peace, love, acceptance, calm, and joy. The presence enveloped me and my joy was indescribable. ... I do not remember re-entering my body.

35. I was sitting on my couch and my breathing was cut off. I was staring at my hand, and I saw myself draw away from my body. Then, something or someone 'pushed' me back into the world. I stood up quickly because I was startled by the whole thing. [Did you meet or see any other beings?] I didn't see or meet anyone or anything, but there was definitely someone else 'there'.

36. I felt like there was someone there but didn't see anything. But something was communicating with me telepathically and every thought was

instant. What the conversation was I don't remember.

37. In shock, I was lying on my bedroom floor when I distinctly heard a male voice say, "Get into bed and whatever happens, do not move, even slightly." I used the last of my strength to get into bed and did not move, couldn't have anyway. At this point, the voice, no longer audible but what I'd call telepathic, instructed me to concentrate on a fuzzy red line in a black void. As long as I concentrated on this flickering red line I'd maintain a foothold to life. ... I realized that I had many agreements for working with people, and that leaving my life would force me to do the whole thing over later, it would selfishly harm a good number of people if I did at that point, and doing the work I needed to do would be much more difficult in another life. In other words, though I had no desire to return to my desiccated, disease-wracked body, I really had no choice in the practical sense. It was the only sensible option to return. The voice accepted my choice and helped me throughout the experience, as needed. I woke up 42 hours later.

38. I realized there was someone or something beside me that calmed my fears somewhat. ... We waited for someone to come. The three others went into ecstasies as a brilliant figure approached. He/it asked me if I wanted to stay there. I thought that my mother would miss me something dreadful if I did not go back. Assent was given.

39. I remember standing (or whatever) in a bright white sort of fog and there was a being (or energy force) on my left. I felt very close to this being (wanting to be with it as one would a spouse, etc.)

40. There was someone I liked beside me, but I sensed them rather than saw them directly and did not know who they were. There were nice sounds around us but I cannot remember what they were like. I really would have liked to stay but I realised I couldn't. I really really had to go.

41. Then I heard a loud voice tell me to put down the drink, stop drinking. I was startled. The voice was very assertive and powerful. I listened and put the drink down. I then felt a window open up in the back of my head and air started rushing through it. I started to feel myself falling, though my friend later stated I was perfectly still. I could still hear the voice. She was telling me I was going to be alright, things were going to be okay, I was safe and didn't need to be scared. I felt very calm even though part of me was terrified of what was happening. I had no control anymore. I couldn't move. I was trying to focus on something to keep me here, but I continued to fall. I could feel my heart stop beating, my body became numb and cold. Everything became dark and suddenly I was falling through a tunnel. It looked very futuristic, like something out of Star Wars, with lights zooming by me at warp speed. I could see images at the end of the tunnel, but none of them were clear enough to distinguish. They

seemed very far away, but no matter how much I kept falling, they never got close enough for me to see. The voice was still reassuring me that everything was going to be alright.

42. There was another there with me, a guide, who was answering my questions. I knew she was female, and had been in her twenties when she died, and she was blonde. I knew that she was my guide on this side. ... My guide had a golden- greenish tinge, like masses of undefined energy. ... I believed that I was going to be there forever. I thought "I'm dead, this is where I will be now." But I felt myself pulled back. No one was more surprised at this than my guide. I believe that she didn't know that I was going back. I felt the heaviness and the disease in my body as I re- entered.

43. Then I remember someone, a being I guess, not really a face just a presence; and, with no words, stopped me in my tracks and let me know I had to go back. It wasn't time yet. The presence gave me the greatest feeling of unconditional love I have ever felt and sent me back without ever speaking a word.

44. I still feel a very real presence was all around me. I was not alone!

45. I became aware of human forms off to my left with one standing right beside me. I could not make out features as it was too bright behind them. The person beside me put out his hand over my crossed hands on my chest and said to me, "You have to go back, your time is not yet." I

argued with him saying that it was to beautiful here and I did not want to go back. He then said "Yes you have to go back, you have a wife and child, you have to go back" .... .

46. I found myself out of my body and in a new environment. A dark haired gentleman met me at the door of a very large complex and invited me in. It wasn't a dream. I remember every detail still, 10 months later. He took me through the building and showed me different areas. He showed me a classroom and I saw a few people sitting at desks. He took me to a room filled with ball gowns and he showed me a rack of them that belonged to me. He took me up on a roof and showed me many people out there. I told him I felt great fear in the people. He said they had come from the September 11th incident and they wouldn't come indoors yet. He took me to a room that looked like a lodge kitchen. It had lots of card tables and a stove and cooking area. There was a grand looking gray-haired man making baked goods. I believe he was the head of the lodge or wherever I was. He looked like a fit Santa Claus. He was very loving and smiled at me. He communicated telepathically. He showed me a vision of my ex- husband hiding stocks in the sand. Then, I was sent back.

47. I also noticed a boy (about in upper teens) waiting by the coffee table. He kept trying to hurry me along with my mom. I kept saying things like (please excuse my French but I'm telling you the whole thing) "---- off and give me

another minute!" ... (The whole time that boy is with me and telling me we had to go). ... I remember being told that I was very much loved and believed in many wrong people and beliefs. I was shown who was true and who was not to me. I was told that I was beautiful and loved and would be missed. One thing I will always remember is being told how my mom was not ready for this. I was shown what would take place if I were not to come back.

48. I'm in another place, walking (floating) with, I think it was, two "beings," for want of a better word. A place of great "light." It is soooooooooooooooooooo beautiful. I feel so wonderful. I feel happy. I feel soooooooooooooooo much love. ... We were walking, floating, over a field of wheat. We were "talking." Much talk. Back and forth. I had sooo many questions. I was soooo happy and at peace. I can't say I felt like these beings were old friends, but I had the feeling of love and safety with them. Again, for want of a better description. We talked and talked and talked as we walked. I kept asking questions, and they kept answering my questions, as we kept walking. I'll mention that our talking was done by thinking. But, it wasn't intruding on one's thoughts. It was just the way we talked. We talked just by asking. But, it was all done without our mouths. The part I find sad, is that I cannot remember one thing that I asked or one thing that they said to me. ... Then they turned to me and told me I had to go back. We

were still in the place of light. I told them I wouldn't go. They tried to convince me to go back. I was adamant. I was staying. Then, another being showed up out of nowhere. I had the feeling he was stronger, or had more authority than the others. Or was different in some way. He talked to me and tried to convince me to return. I still refused, and was steadfast in my decision. I was staying, and they couldn't do anything about it. I was staying. All of a sudden, there was this force pulling me backward. I resisted with all my might, but it was no use. It was stronger than I was. I kept being pulled backward. It was quick. I woke up in my body.

49. I "communicated" with "something" that I did not really see, but it was there and told me that I had to return. I remember that I wanted to stay. (I did not feel any connection with my family and found it completely irrelevant as an argument to return.) It was not my time and I had still to do something on earth. Without telling me what and so, I still ask myself what I have to do. But, it will be clear when the time is there as I was told. Before sending me back I was allowed to ask something and I remember very well. I asked how the universe was composed and it was explained to me in all details. I remember that it was extremely beautiful and extremely simple and said to myself this information I must remember when I am sent back. Being sent back, I remember very well that it was a very painful experience to be put in a tunnel that becomes

more and more narrow, and also when dimensions more and more became restricted. I lost control over the information I got earlier (it felt as if my head was crashed). I woke up in my bed and found the earth a terrible dark place that really frightened me at that moment.

50. Then I am seeing a woman (she is beautiful with long brown hair) at the end of my hospital bed, and I can see myself lying in the bed. I am confused. I look at her and I am speaking to her and I don't know how because I can see myself in the hospital bed with tubes down my throat, hooked to machines. I am trying to convey to her the dream I had but she already knows and asks me while smiling: "Did you see the light?" I answer "yes." I look at myself in the hospital bed, then look back towards her and she is gone. Then I wake up.

51. I had a very odd feeling sweep through my body; it started at my feet and moved up. I knew I was in trouble. I tried to scream. I saw a woman by my bed.

52. I was also not alone, there was a being behind me coaching me as what to say to my brother. I watched as they put me on the stretcher and carried me down the stairs, they were hurrying, and my body was flopping around. I thought that was funny, until I saw my face. I looked peaceful. Now I was afraid. I turned to the being and he pointed for me to look, as I did I saw the ambulance driving away. I saw the doctor put a tube in my mouth. I couldn't hear any more now

but, the being wanted me to watch. I felt a pull, a strong pull from beyond where I was, I didn't want to go. The being pointed and no words but I could hear it speak, "go now, you are not done." The pull hurt like being slammed into a wall. I woke up 3 days latter strapped to the bed.

53. I began to feel a presence beside me. I didn't look to the side, because I didn't need to—I knew it was God. I said, "God, who's going to raise my babies?" There was a bright flash of light—like I was in the middle of a lightning bolt—and then I don't remember anything until the next day. I opened my eyes and saw bottles and IVs hanging above my bed.

54. I was "dead" for eight minutes and CPR had to be performed. I remember a man in a hat. He was standing in the doorway, almost leaning a bit with his arms crossed. He was just looking at me but I could not really make out a face. He was pleasant and I felt comfortable with him. We talked, but at this point I can't remember much of the conversation. He came and went over the next few days. I was not sleeping much because I was waiting for him. My mother happened to be there and she told me that a pastor had come and spoke with me, and I do remember him, but they were getting confused when I spoke of the man in the hat. I would tell them about meeting with him and they would assume that I was talking about the pastor. I spent over 40 days in the hospital. When I went home I had other visions of him but kept them to myself. I don't know why.

55. I dozed off. When I woke up, I saw a guy sitting at the end of my bed; I couldn't see the face. I thought it was my dad so I said "Dad," and he looked around... He was faceless! The guy had NO FACE! I screamed. He got up and said to me "come with me" and put his hand forward. I was screaming and refused to go but to my amazement I was moving. We both started flying and up we went. I realized I was up near the hospital roof and could see myself lying on the bed down below. Next thing...we were in a dark eerie place. I was standing in a pew with a few people. Then someone pushed the two ladies in the front in a ball of fire. The guy who pushed them was so tall, dark and very scary. We moved to another pew and 2 people were pushed to a BIG SHARK who started eating them. I saw big glasses breaking etc. Then next I know is, I was back on the hospital roof. I could see lots of nurses and doctors around my body doing something. I started falling down, and in I went into my body!

56. All the time there was a being with me, I realized that it always had been with me! But it was disappointed in me. I had the choice to go into that tunnel, but I felt my life would be a failure if I had chosen to do that.

57. I felt a presence next to me now. I could not see anyone but somehow I knew someone was there. ... I could still feel the presence of someone next to me, almost as if they were mentally telling me where to look next.

58. I do remember being with three others, one in the middle was a little above the two, on one side was my brother, who died at 11days, the other was my grandpa. I don't know how we got there, but it was such a beautiful color blue surrounding, not ground but not like we were hovering. We talked a lot, but I can't remember our mouths moving. I paid [attention] mostly to my brother, his clothes, his hair, how tall, but cannot remember the one in the middle. I know he said a lot to me, but I don't know what. My sister says when I first opened my eyes I said "God says I'm a ●●●●● and won't let me stay."

59. As I was floating towards the tree I could hear a voice say, "You can't go now." I stopped and looked around, but I don't remember seeing anyone, but I felt someone. I remember saying, but not speaking, "I don't want to leave." I could hear the voice in my head saying, "Not now, your children need you, look up." I looked up and I could see my two children and my husband reaching over a mountain trying to grab my hand. I seem like I was at the bottom of this steep cliff. The voice told me to go but don't let the hands touch me. At that moment I began to raise up the side of the cliff. I then notice hands started to reach out of the cliff. Just as I was almost at the top, I could see my family reaching for me, and all of a sudden I felt as though I was pushed up and over, and I woke up.

60. This is not the only time I have had a near-death experience. ... I remember laying on the

bed, and all of a sudden I was in this very bright place full of warmth and love. I was not alone. I could feel someone on both sides of me, and we were approaching this person with two other persons on each side of that person. I felt as though this person was both male and female. As I got closer I could see white. Each person on the sides were very important to the person in the middle, and there was love. The person in the middle had on a bright white robe, and I remember seeing gold ropes hanging from the waist of this person, but I could never see a face. As I approached and stood in front of this person I felt incredible love. I did not want to leave, but I could hear this person say, "Breathe." Just as this was said to me, I took a deep breath and woke up.

61. Then I heard what I thought was a lady's voice. The pitch was soft and gentle, was I dreaming? I couldn't hear clearly. I just had to get closer so I could comprehend exactly what the voice was saying so I started going toward the tone of the feminine voice. Not really walking, more like drifting, yet not really floating as such. As I got closer I could hear the words this lady was speaking to a figure of a man next to her. She kept saying, "There she is. Oh! Isn't she lovely. Look at her." I felt as though I knew her, yet didn't. I couldn't see her clearly nor the man standing to her left but I could make out the shapes of two shadow people, an older woman and a young man. As I got even closer to them,

the lady kept saying, "No go back as your Mammy needs you." I couldn't understand what was going on. I just wanted to go with them. It seemed such a happy place to be therefore I kept going forward. However, the lady insisted that I go back as, "Mammy needed me." I didn't really want to go back through the dark, however, somehow I was turned back.

62. I would open my eyes in the hospital bed and a blue-eyed wolf was next to me. I don't remember getting out of my bed, but I would go down a hall with the wolf. We would get to a door and somehow the wolf opened the door. A blond woman, wearing white was on the other side. I never saw her face. She and the wolf led me down a long dark tunnel. She was on my right and the wolf on my left. I remember holding onto the wolf's fur. I never saw a bright light. At the end of the tunnel, the woman opened a door and I walked out to a large field. It was beautiful. There were trees, flowers, and many birds. There were a lot of people, but it did not seem crowded. I walked up a small hill and sat with a woman who had short dark hair. She was sitting with her knees pulled up and arms wrapped around her knees. We talked. I can't remember anything we said. When it was my time to leave, I knew I would walk back to the door. The woman and the wolf were there and walked me back through the tunnel. Once through the other door, the wolf would take me back to my room. I had this experience more than once because I remember

feeling so relieved when I would open my eyes and the wolf would be there. That is why I was trying to go back later. I realized that I could not go back on my own and could only go back if the wolf took me.

63. Some were being welcomed with open arms and carefully guided through the transition point and into the wonderful light of the white tunnel; some were being greeted with discussions; and some were being turned back toward the earth plane. When I was met by my own entourage of souls, I could clearly see that they were human, but in this existence were beings of light. They seemed to be the same colour as the electric blue in the first tunnel. I was greeted with a great love and urgency. I was held, and knowledge was imbued into me.

64. The person who was watching me walked across the bridge and said goodbye to me.

65. Then I felt something wrap around me (draped over my shoulders). A voice came into my ear saying, "Cindy ask him to forgive you." I said, "Oh Lord forgive me." The voice came into my ear again saying, "Now Cindy ask him to help you." I did. At the same time while moving toward the light I heard my mother saying, "Cindy please don't leave me like this." I was in a great hurry to get to this light, and the closer I came to it the more the brightness took over the door. I couldn't get there fast enough. Almost entering the light, the voice came again and said, "Cindy you have a short time." I was so mad

because I didn't get to stay and remember being mad for several days after that. I opened my eyes and saw my family and asked them if I died. My sister said, "No, you're okay now." I said, "No I died." Then I proceeded to tell them what happened to me.

66. A voice up in front and to my right said, "Fear not. Do not be afraid." My uneasy feeling went away as I asked, "Who are you?" The voice answered, "Just call me father." In the center of my being I heard, "Christ." Then before me there were images, fuzzy and dark like the scene of the car with my friend and I below. ... Suddenly, I was standing in my mother's bedroom. The dog woke up and I said, "Hampton, it is okay." Then the voice up, in back, and to my right asked, "Is this not your mother?" I said, "Yes." Then my vision was turned to the right where I would see through my younger brother's door. The voice asked, "Is this not your brother?" I said, "Yes." Then in the blink of an eye I was 12 miles away outside my older brother's apartment. Looking down through the concrete floor of the second story and the steel security door of his apartment, I could see my brother reaching out to open the apartment door. Beside him was a shadowy figure. The voice up, behind me, and to the right said, "Is this not your other brother." Thinking that I could talk to the dog, and that my brother is awake, I started to say, "Charles. Get me out of this. Charles. Get me out of this." The voice again said in a monotone voice, "Is this not

your other brother?" Again, I said, "Charles. Get me out of this." Then the voice said in a fainter voice, "Is this not your other brother?" I said, "Yes." Then again in the blink of an eye I was taken 15 miles away to my father's apartment. I was hovering in the parking lot looking at him through his apartment door while he sat on the couch reading a newspaper. I was looking through

the newspaper at his face when I wondered about his wife. I was told that she was in the bedroom. Then I was asked, "Is this not your father?" I said, "Yes." In an instant, I was back in the darkness where I saw the 360-degree vision. The last one- quarter was quickly scanned. Then I had a sense of front and back. There were voices in a murmur behind me as if eight to 10 people were all talking at once. The voice up and to the right told me something and then to look behind me and to my right. I saw an image of myself in a white robe as if it were hanging on a coat hook. My head bowed down. My right hand held my left wrist at arms length and rested on my belly. As I turned forward, I could sense that the voice was gone.

67. Then I didn't hear a voice, but rather I was asked a question by this entity. It told me if I wanted to come out now I could, or I could go back. No voice, but I felt the question in a big way. I thought of my life and fiancée and decided to go back. Right then I opened my eyes and was still on the rolling gurney, almost in the very

same spot as if no time had passed at all. ... All of a sudden I was off the planet and floating way above the earth, although I could feel it behind me. I was looking into a star field, a massive, infinite entity that encompassed all of the galaxies, all of space, and some presence which is right in front of us all of the time that the earth sits in. It was massive and unimaginable. And, I had the thought that all of the dark matter and dark energy in the whole of the void was God. I was overwhelmed by the size of this presence. I understood that it knew everything about me as if it had built me cell by cell.

68. I was in a hospital bed in a clinical room that wasn't solid. To my left stood my yoga teacher's wife, Bha, who had died three years previously of breast cancer. Bha was talking animatedly with a blue light being; he was tall and the shape of a man, but he had no features. A neon turquoise blue light outlined his shape and he had lights moving on the inside of his shape like sunlight playing on water. Bha and the light being were laughing a lot. I was aware that my lungs weren't moving and I was trying to make my chest go up and down by breathing; nothing was happening. Bha came over and said, "Stop interfering, let the machine breathe for you, all you have to do is be here." I thought I would give it a go and stopped trying to breathe, I realised that I was still here even if I didn't breathe. ... I was back in the room with Bha and the light being. Bha said, "It's time for you to go back now." I said I didn't want to go

back. A vision came into my mind of my daughter crying over my grave. I could feel what my daughter was feeling and I thought, "Ah, she's not ready for me to leave her yet. I'd better go back." As soon as I had the thought, I was back in my body. ... For some years, I would wake at about 2 a.m. and the blue being (Michael) would teach me spiritual things until about 5 a.m. Although I still sense him around me, his presence is not as evident in my life as it was. This has been my choice because I felt that I was becoming too dependent on him to guide me. ... I went into a flow of oneness that I think is God, (I called that the "isness"); it is a state of bliss where I am all there is. It is formless. It is like waking from a nightmare and finding yourself safe at home. Life on earth is the dream and this oneness/bliss is the reality that you wake up into safe and sound.

69. I was engulfed in a beautiful light. It was all around me and it was composed of unimaginable kindness. It was like being in the middle of the sun. I delighted the sun. It knew what I was like— faults and all, but it loved me completely. It was also horrified by what I had done; that is, I had gone there alone and unaided. It didn't know a human being could do that. ... As I walked around inside the sun, I became aware that there was someone else walking around with me. I didn't recognize this person, but I was aware that he was unique and loved me. ... I was walking across a grassy heath with one other person. He was dressed like a soldier or as if prepared for an

arduous journey. I was wearing a long, white dress, which was some sort of a mark of distinction. We had been very happy in our time together and we had agreed to meet again.

70. From ages three to eight, I had an "imaginary" friend I named Mr. Cardine. He would take me to places outside my body and tell me what was going to happen to me and other family members. I could also see other beings, but I could not see Mr. Cardine. When I would be out of my body, I could see people having conversations and I could listen to their plans. It was very hard to understand why other people did not believe me when I would tell them what was going to happen. Mr. Cardine was very friendly and never frightened me. I thought everyone knew Mr. Cardine and I would talk about him to everyone. Soon I was the target of ridicule and bullying because nobody believed my stories or that I had an "imaginary" friend. My mother got frightened because I was telling her things that happened and were going to happen. Her concern for my behavior prompted her to go to a preacher in the Holiness denomination and he began to tell me that Mr. Cardine was not real. I would tell him things about his life and he told mother to take me to a doctor. The doctor told me to kill Mr. Cardine and my parents wanted me to tell them when he dies. One day while I was talking to some of the other beings, mother got angry and gave me a spanking and then dad did the same when he got home. Mr. Cardine was the

main being in that realm of existence. He could make all the others leave. I could not hear his voice or see him; it was a presence I would feel and the communication was verbal on my part, but I am not sure how I understood him. I would see many other beings too. Some of them looked like melted piles of tar and I was very afraid of them. They were able to move through walls and I could tell that they had no boundaries, as I knew boundaries. I remember their presence mostly when my parents were arguing or drinking and arguing. Mr. Cardine could make the tar-like beings leave. The last time I was aware of Mr. Cardine was the day I had to tell my parents he had fallen off the roof, broke his leg and died. He told me to do this and said he would always be with me but I could not talk to him anymore because of the beatings my parents started giving me when they caught me talking to him. Fast forward to my 39th year. It was 1995 on July 14th that my life changed. I had been breaking out in hives for 21 years and I didn't know what caused it. I ate a peanut butter sandwich and five minute later I could feel the hives starting. One hive was below my navel and it was worse than any hive I had ever had. In the mirror I watched the hive move around my body in a circle that ended back at the origin of the hive. At that time my body felt as I it was on fire. I knew I needed to get to the hospital immediately. When I got to the hospital I was very faint feeling and I walked in the ambulance door and the staff nurse told me to go to admissions and fill out the forms. I told her I could hardly stand up anymore and requested a wheelchair. After arguing for a few minutes she agreed to take my information. I was seated in front of her and after a few questions I told her I needed to lie down. I heard her saying something and I laid on the floor. The next thing I knew I was floating above my body and watching it as people were giving me CPR. I heard a voice that said, "Why have you worried so much in your life?" I looked at my body again. The voice said, "What good is it now?" I turned to see who was talking and the ceiling was not a barrier to me anymore. I went through to the outside and I looked in the night sky for the voice's origin. I did not recognize it at first and I found myself focused on a star. The star started to get large and I was enveloped in its light. I looked toward the source of the light and saw the light was coming from a core of colors that were in an oval shape and swirling around in beautiful patterns. Somehow the colors started to form a space and I knew I was supposed to go in that space. I then recognized the voice as it said, "Here is your assured home you built while you were living. Have you finished everything you want in this life?" I thought about my woodcarvings that were not finished. I found myself back in my body that instant. I could feel the weight of the nurse sitting on my chest and compressing my heart. I said, "What in the hell am I doing back here?" I was then moved to a cubical with a doctor. He started inserting tubes into my arm and talking to me. He asked me, "How are you feeling?" and to stay awake and not close my eyes. I relaxed and I heard the voice of Mr. Cardine. He said, "This is what happens to evil people." Then I saw a man I had never seen before. He had a look of terror in his eyes that seemed to convey that he saw where he was going and why. He then turned to a cloud of light that was colorful light swirling about in the center of the cloud. I suddenly saw one of the tar-like beings and the cloud formed a point that drew the whole cloud into the tar-like being. I saw a woman do the same and several others came in rapid succession. Mr. Cardine said, "This will happen to your mother." I awoke suddenly on the stretcher with the doctor yelling for me to hang on. He said, "You have to hang on, don't close your eyes." I said, "What in the hell am I doing back here again." I was on the stretcher and a moment later Mr. Cardine said, "We are going on a journey." I saw the composition of the ceiling materials and I found myself moving in darkness. I wasn't afraid because Mr. Cardine was there. We came upon something I do not know how to describe other than to say it was the largest thing I ever knew. It was alive and knew I was there. It was communicating with Mr. Cardine but I could not understand them. We started moving again and suddenly we stopped in the presence of another larger being, larger than the first. They both turned from each other and looked at me. I have never felt anything so good. I felt love. I tried to say something but I was not able to communicate at all. Mr. Cardine and I were suddenly moving and the last thing I heard him say was, "You have chosen life. You will suffer as you help others." I awoke to the doctor's yelling for me to hold on and wake up. He was slapping me and I said, "What in the hell am I doing back here?"

71. I could see myself lying on the bed. There was somebody beside me, but I couldn't see a face. I wasn't frightened of him. I saw the doctor who was stitching my head turn to the other doctor, say something, then I saw him put his hand in his top pocket. Then I was in another room, with the person still beside me.

72. Calming voice told me that everything would be explained when I arrived. I trusted this voice. Arriving at the end of the tunnel I was greeted by a man who looks pretty much like I do today. He brought me to the edge of whatever I was standing on and when I looked into the inky blackness, all sense of time vanished. There was no past, present or future. Only everything all at once. I felt a tremendous understanding of the nature of the universe and my place in it. He showed me what looked like a huge white obelisk floating in the blackness. As I looked at it more closely, I saw that the surface was moving. It was a giant puzzle and it looked like it was being solved. He showed me my place and how the puzzle was re-arranged with each action by anyone on earth. Some of the puzzle had already

fallen into place and I knew that something wonderful was going to happen when it was complete. Of course, I don't remember what it is but I still look forward to it! I was then sent back to my body.

73. In the beginning I was walking somewhere and it was dark, it looks like a different town or city. Someone is with me but I cannot see who.

74. Just as I had started walking around this waiting area, something lifted me off the ground. I stumbled over something down under the smoky area. I was inside of it, up to my knees, then I was lifted up onto my back again. I had heard this wonderful, familiar voice, "It is not yet your time to be here. You must go back." I begged it to please not send me back. And that is when it told me I had a mission to do. I begged it to please tell me the mission so I could do it and come back. Then it told me I had to go back and perform my mission when the time came. I would not know what it was until that time. Then it would be my time to be there. I awoke in the hospital.

75. The Being quickly asked me what the thought was that had just entered my consciousness. I had thought that it would be a shame for my daughters to have grown up without their father in their life. I had spent a large part of my life without my father in it, and I would have liked my daughters not to experience that. Anyway, I was ready to go. The Being said that because my reason for wanting to return was somebody

outside myself, I would be allowed to return. Before I had the chance to express that I didn't really want to return, there was a rapid, confused movement, something happened, the other spark which had been "observing" was somehow a part of it, and then I was waking up in this body.

LOVE FROM THE GUIDES

1. I was very sharp and aware, and in the presence of an intelligence that adored me, or so it seemed.

2. I was like a baby wrapped in love. But the love was so intense, I did wonder a little about it I think. It felt new. Like a rebirth.

3. As Jesus held me, I looked into his eyes—I will never forget how wonderful and awesome his eyes were! The first thing I said to him was, "Do you hate me because I am a drug Addict?" I will never forget what He said to me: "No, I only want you to know that I love you." There were other things said and then he started to set me down and I said, "Please don't leave me," and HE said, "I will never give you more than you can handle." Then I was back in my body.

4. As he sat me on his lap and laid in his arms, I reached up and touched his beard with my right hand and felt the most immense sense of love and understanding. Until this day this feeling has never left me.

5. Suddenly, I saw this beautiful white light slowly coming towards me. A man who had a kind gentle face dressed in a white cloth was before me. He stood to the right side of this ever-growing light. While I began to move in his direction, he was so welcoming and only spoke to me it seemed through his eyes. He asked me if I wanted to enter the light. I was overjoyed that he

had come for me and loved me so much. I can't really describe the joy or calm I felt. I wanted to go with him so badly.

6. I detest using the word "God," because of the great perversion we humans have made of the concept, but I will use it from this point onward, merely for the sake of expedience. I was "sitting in God's lap," wrapped in the warmest embrace, and immediately involved in a "conversation." ... My field of vision was akin to being inside a TV screen watching a movie. The movie kept running, the road kept going...so fast...so much "information." Personal, universal. Mostly about Thought and Love. ... The totality of God's love for me was the predominant feeling/understanding, at all times (luckily, that feeling has stayed with me, though I don't necessarily understand it, any more) ... .

7. Amidst some commotion, through the back came Jesus Christ, and there was no mistake as to who he was; he looked like the artist's portraits, but not meek and mild, as often portrayed, he was healthy and robust. He put his arm around me, in the area of what would have been my shoulder, looked me straight in the eyes and said "I have come for you, that you may know that I am real." I was totally awestruck by His presence, yet I felt a love and respect for Him that I have never felt in physical life.

8. I was aware of a presence that was at once familiar and loving and kind and all powerful and so very immense that there will never be any

words appropriate to describe this thing. My first thought was, "It knows my name!" I was in awe that this amazing force knew me! It was exciting and exhilarating that something so immense an important took the effort to know little me.

9. I glanced up, an indescribable "light", like an opening to another dimension, to a completely different world. And there was a face. I will never forget that face! It was so full of a welcoming, a non-demanding, warm smile of love. In that inviting face, as in the whole experience, there was nothing else than a complete pure and total love, unlimited comprehension, kindness, and real affectionate, sympathetic and warm humour.

10. At this time I was being pulled at a high rate of speed and there was somebody with me and I felt safe and loved and at peace.

11. Then I heard encouraging voices behind my head saying so gently and lovingly, "Come on. It's OK."

12. There was an unseen 'someone' approaching me. An indescribable overwhelming love began to completely envelope me, and with it came a sense of joy that defies words.

13. Jesus was really there. ... He put His Arm around me. He loved me.

14. The presence was unbelievable peace, love, acceptance, calm, and joy. The presence enveloped me and my joy was indescribable.

15. A radiant being in long white robes was there to greet me. I could not discern the sex of the being, or the face of the being. However the most

incredible feeling of love surrounded me. It emanated from the being. We were communicating through mental telepathy. I have never experienced such joy.

16. Then I looked to the sky and saw an image of a smiling woman with wavy golden hair. Underneath her were stalks of golden wheat. She was glowing, emanating beauty, peace and love.

17. The presence gave me the greatest feeling of unconditional love I have ever felt and sent me back without ever speaking a word.

18. Then soon I'm in another place, walking (floating) with, I think it was, two "beings," for want of a better word. A place of great "light". It is soooooooooooooooooo beautiful. I feel so wonderful. I feel happy. I feel soooooooooooooooo much love. It is indescribable. There is so much love. The outstanding feature of this entire experience is the feeling (?), knowing (?), no, it's the love itself. A love I've never experienced on this earth. Never in my earthly life have I experienced the pure love. Not pure love. Maybe it was pure love. Or maybe it was "full" love of which we experience only minute aspects of it on earth. ... I can't say I felt like these beings were old friends, but I had the feeling of love and safety with them.

19. I "passed out." During this period I went to a place which was very loving. All communication was telepathic. There was a complete dialogue between myself and this unknown source.

20. After closing my eyes, the next recollection was myself being in the presence of, in the arena of, enveloped in, PURE UNCONDITIONAL LOVE. A communication occurred, through instantaneous osmosis, rather than our human verbalization.

21. I began to feel a presence beside me. I didn't look to the side, because I didn't need to—I knew it was God. I felt comforted and loved ... .

22. After the exchange with the beings of light, I felt myself float up and over the room. I now felt like I was warm and very loved and very happy to be there.

23. I realized there was someone right in front of me. The clouds also thickened around that shadow so I could not see him. There are no words to describe the incredibly intense love I felt, standing there in front of him. No one could ever imagine a love so powerfully strong. At that moment, it hit me. I was in heaven standing before our Lord. ... If I could only choose one word to describe our Lord, it would have to be "Love", an indisputable love. I don't know how to explain it. I couldn't see Him through the clouds and light, but I felt His love so deeply.

24. The feeling was of endless body and carefree, loving and worry free. Then, I felt something "push" me back down.

25. The feeling around me was the most loving feeling and the sun was shining soooo bright, but it was not hot, it was warm, just right. I could see in the distance, a tree, a large tree, and I remember I had to go toward it. As I was floating

towards the tree I could hear a voice say, "You can't go now." I stopped and looked around, but I don't remember seeing anyone, but I felt someone.

26. Someone or something was holding me to their chest like a baby. Even though I could not make out faces or forms, I just knew I loved, loved, loved. There are no words for the feelings of love I received and felt. This was no earthly experience, that is for sure!

27. Behind me became bright and I saw a hand.

28. When I first saw him I felt as though I knew him. I hugged him; the love I had for him was very strong. He felt closer to me than my own family.

29. I remember being in a beautiful garden with huge flowers and big colorful butterflies. Someone in all white escorted me to this place, and there were other children there. I remember running and playing with them and nobody seemed to be different because the love was so strong.

30. I was warm, loved, peaceful, and perfect, something I thought I knew until that night. It made no difference in love between my wife and the strangers, yet I knew I had a connection.

31. Then a voice spoke over my left shoulder, a voice so beautiful, full of love and so deep that I will never forget that sound.

32. We started moving again and suddenly we stopped in the presence of another larger being, larger than the first. They both turned from each

other and looked at me. I have never felt anything so good. I felt love.

33. When Jesus and I talked it wasn't with our mouths, but I knew we were communicating. His countenance fairly shone, and how he felt about me shone forth about him. He simply exuded love and concern and caring for me, just by standing there. The feeling of peace I felt was indescribable.

34. I noticed the angel was still along side me. It seems that he knows exactly why I am here. ... The peace was absolutely overwhelming. I felt like I could burst at any moment because of the intense love that streamed through me.

35. Then a calming voice communicated into my mind the thought, "Yes, but its okay." Then I am immersed, engulfed by total love.

36. Some entity like none I've ever encountered was embracing me. Complete unconditional love and acceptance.

37. I found my self surrounded by PURE LOVE and I felt as if I was being embraced by Jesus. I cannot tell you what he looked like but I knew who I was with. ... I remember seeing my life review and I was ashamed but when I turned to Christ I was greeted with pure love and I was guiltless.

38. I then sensed a presence. I had the knowledge that this was Jesus, and he was assuring me that everything was fine. I felt total love from this presence.

39. Anyway, to my right was someone very awesome, a male. This big love seemed related to this being. I didn't know who it was but I was very awestruck.

40. Three men. ... As I neared the men the one facing me reached out and placed his hand on my left forearm and spoke to me, saying, "Don't pay any attention to them. Everything is fine, you are with me now". I turned back to these men and my heart became so full of love and warmth and joy that words can't begin to describe how good I felt.

41. I remember feeling as if a tremendous burden had been lifted from me, and remember a sense of another presence. ... Then there was an intense sense of well being, a feeling like immersion in the emotions of love, surrounding from every point.

42. I arrived in an explosion of glorious light into a room with insubstantial walls, standing before a man about in his 30's about 6 feet tall, reddish brown shoulder length hair and an incredibly neat, short beard & mo. He wore a simple white robe, light seemed to emanate from Him and I felt He had great age and wisdom. He welcomed me with great love, tranquility, peace (indescribable), no words.

43. I told the Being that I knew was there, and had to be God, that I couldn't die. And then a voice, not heard with my ears, but somehow within my head, said, "Don't be afraid, you will not die.

GUIDES INTERVENE IN PHYSICAL LIFE?

1. I remember being the only car on the road. I dozed off for a moment, and when I opened my eyes, I saw a dark black puff of smoke hit my windshield and then it vanished. Then the next thing I remember was that I was moving in slow motion across an open field of green grass. ... Something telling me that I have a reason to live. That I was put on this earth for a reason.

2. I came onto the bridge, lost control of my car, thought I would die, saw my life pass in front of me. And at that same moment, something intervened to redirect my car and I glided safely to the other side. The next day, I took a walk near the bridge to study the icy effects and discover details. The bridge was closed. Someone else had gone over it after me, lost control and did not survive.

3. I felt something (what I know now was an angel) wrap around my arms and legs. I started being pulled back into my body when I was overwhelmed with the feeling of peace and calm. I knew that I was in an accident, that I was being protected, and that I would survive.

4. It was snowing big flakes around 8 at night. We were under way to tow two barges to Toronto. As we pulled up to the barges I jumped off to connect the batteries to the running lights and I heard a yell back at the tug. The engineer was looking down and that's when I saw Rick coming

up to the surface. As the decks were slippery with snow as soon as I grabbed him I was in danger of being pulled in. So the first mate grabbed a hold of my legs. The tug was getting closer, and as Rick's head was going to get it, I couldn't let him go. I squared my shoulders and thought that maybe I'd just break a shoulder. Well the tug just kept on coming and I knew it had to stop soon, but by then I realized I couldn't get out if I tried. At first I thought my ribs were going to cave in, and then I said goodbye to my family and I thought my head was going to pop off. Then a friend from back home in Glen was right beside me. Bruce and he said, "It's okay relax, you're welcome." He was guiding me towards the most brilliant light and a roaring tunnel. In my mind I asked what was happening? A voice came. A male voice just kind of matter-of-factly said, "You are drowning." Instantly, I saw my mother and my two little sisters Mary-Lou and Lorna crying at the kitchen table like I never want to see anybody like that again. I yelled out, "No!" And not knowing where I was I just started kicking. I don't know how but when I hit the surface of the water and took my first breath, I still didn't know where I was. As it was still snowing all was dark. I must have been facing south towards Lake Huron east towards Bush, north twenty miles up South Bay mouth, west, and I could make out a bit of light and I dog- paddled toward the light. Getting near the stern of a tugboat, I read the name Flo Cooper. I swam up the side and could hear the engines. I realized I worked on it. Swimming around the bow I heard voices and the chief yelled out, "McRae," and my name came back. Rick was holding onto a ladder that was tied off to the barge but he couldn't get his feet up to the first rung. So I reached up to grab the ladder. First time I felt pain in my shoulders. Got hold of the ladder and with my head under Rick's butt end boosted him up to the barge. I climbed up after and just remember looking up into the snow coming down through the lights. The captain was giving me shit for going in the water, and we changed our gear and went back to work. As I was on shift till midnight the only thing I remember was how hard it was turn the big steering wheel.

5. I was doing around 70 - 80mph. I knew I was going to crash and that I was going to die. Even though I knew death was inevitable I remained remarkably calm, and time seemed to almost stop, as though everything was happening in slow motion. The next thing I knew I was in darkness watching a detailed review of my life up to that point in my life. It was like watching a huge cinema screen in 3D and it was incredibly detailed in that it literally covered every event in my life. I remembered events, people and places that I had long forgotten. It was as if I was effectively reliving my entire life although it was done at high speed. I sensed there were beings around me (although I did not actually see them) and they made it clear that they were not judging

any part of my life. I got the impression that this was my life, that I should observe it and then consider any aspects that I wished to discuss. Once I absorbed this information I was then informed that it was not my time and that I should return. I was loathe to do so as I had a feeling of such absolute calm, love and peace which is simply not possible to describe. The next thing I knew I was back in the car driving along as if nothing had happened and saying to myself that this was not possible. It seemed the passengers in the car were totally unaware of what had happened. It was as if any memory had been erased from their minds.

6. I was in an auto on an icy road. I went through frozen, unable to move. ... I was accompanied by a voice that repeated my own words and others in my past. I felt the car move under me and saw it from the sky, looking down. I saw and heard a strange vector of air and sound that wasn't from the event unfolding before my eyes, and right before I was put back in my auto with my friend who was riding in the passenger seat, I was asked by a person who's image was blurred, "do you want to return?"

7. I looked again at my car traveling to the other side of the freeway. I puzzled why it was moving. Suddenly a man's voice in my right ear stated, "If you don't go back, someone will die." I remember not wanting that to happen. I woke up with my hands on the steering wheel and trying to gain

control of the car and trying to turn it away from the oncoming traffic. I eventually came to a stop.

8. My car was on fire, and I couldn't get out of the door because my car was leaning sideways. A man who was about 5'4" and 140lbs came running to my side. He had a cleanly trimmed beard, a soft voice and strong hands. ... He lifted me out of the window as though I were a child and carried me away from the fire. He sat me down and said I would be alright now. Everything was going to be ok. He reminded me of my grandfather in a strange way. One I cannot describe. When the firemen and police arrived the man disappeared and I have never seen him since. There is no account of this man, no one saw him, and I don't even know if he was real. But to me he was very real. He pulled me from a burning wreckage, he saved my life.

9. I first fall in a kind of waterhole with my feet forward. Then I decide to take the path towards death, with the light at the end. I think of my life and my family. My son of five years old appears. He is an angel that smiles to me. How will he be doing without his father? I have to climb up, I cannot. But a hand grabs me. I don't see a face. He helps me to turn my head upwards where life is and I climb up and get out.

10. I was on a motorcycle at about 90mph in a two-lane road when out came a car from my right side and in front of me. I went from the right lane to the left lane as fast as I could and then realized that so did the car. As I applied the brakes there

was a sprinkler on which was spraying half the road and I was on that half. The bike didn't slow down at all and somehow did not even fall over. It just stayed its course. At this point I was sure I was going to die. That's when I felt myself float away at about 15 feet to the right and close to the ground looking at myself on the motorcycle about 5 feet from the rear bumper of the car I was about to hit. As I see myself I notice that behind my head was my life flashing in fast motion backwards. I was able to focus on that and can remember some but most of all I remember seeing myself as a baby being held by a woman, I'm assuming is my mother. Then actually seeing through that baby's eyes what seemed to be what it first saw when those eyes opened up after birth. At that point I was then back on my bike and saw the car in front of me with my headlights shining on the rear of the chrome bumper. As I was just about to hit I felt myself being lifted to where I was almost standing up. Then from the impact I was going forward, which all seemed like slow motion. I saw and felt my head going through the rear windshield. That's when everything turned black and I felt myself floating. I was able to open my eyes to see but couldn't make out what was in front of me. Then I looked down at myself to see if I was in one piece and noticed I couldn't see myself but what I did see was a shadow of myself with my arms to my sides but up. As I was looking at myself I noticed I was not alone. All around me were other shapes very similar to mine and others different all moving forward. So I looked to see where we were moving to and that's when I saw this very bright light far away. I seemed to be in some sort of ray of light going in its direction. When I saw this light the most peaceful feeling came over me that can never be described in human words. All I wanted to do was go to the light. What seemed so far away I reached in less than a second without the feeling of movement. As I was about to go into the light with even a more wonderful feeling, I noticed something below me and to the right. As I glanced over I noticed it was my mother's father who died years earlier looking at me waving his arms in a do not enter movement so I stopped in my tracks, like superman can do in his movies, and stared at my grandfather. I can't remember if he was trying to say something or not but I did not hear anything. I just knew he was telling me to stop. That's when my vision became very bright and white but my eyes stayed open. Then my body felt different, like my weight was back. It seemed like I was trying to close my eyes from the brightness but I was actually opening them. I remember feeling very confused about that but then my eyes opened and I saw that I was sitting on top of a car which was moving with my legs straight out and my upper body was in an upward position (sitting) with my back completely erect and my arms to my sides holding myself up. When I saw this I tried to move but could not for a couple of seconds then slowly I could. Without questioning my self, I jumped off the car and slid into oncoming traffic watching cars swerve around me. Then I stood up and saw the bike I crashed about 80 yards away.

11. I was driving the family station wagon in the mountains in December, it was starting to rain and I had not been driving long. The engine died and the car locked up and I lost control. The car went end over end twice and rolled about 7 times. The witness to the accident said he did not know how anyone survived the accident. My 15 year old brother and his friend were also in the front seat. None of us had our seat belts on, but I was the only one injured. While the car was rolling, at first everything went black and it got very cold. All of a sudden it became very warm, a nice warm, and a light started to appear before me. In the light my father started to appear to me and seemed to hold out his hand, as if to motion me to come with him. It was such a nice feeling that I wanted to go. My father was smiling as if to say everything was alright. My father appeared to me only from the waist up, and there was this warm light all around him. But after a couple of minutes his image disappeared and I realized where I was. I only received a bad gash behind my left ear. I did [not] have to even stay in the hospital except to get stitches. To this day I cannot explain what happened.

12. I saw the light of the truck coming at our car and heard a bang. I was then above a street light watching the car flip over and over to rest on the sidewalk. Then I saw greyish cement-looking material and thought I was in a conduit of some kind. I was quite afraid and felt very cold I wanted to get out. Then I sensed I was moving and the cement-like conduit started to speed past my eyes. I was scared but turned and looked ahead and saw a light and was increasing with greater and greater speed until I left the conduit into brilliant white light which was extremely bright but not hard on the eyes. I did not know where I was but soon sensed that I was not alone. I then saw what I can best describe as an opaque window or screen. Like a shower curtain. I saw silhouettes of sorts and sensed that it was my mother who died in 1971, my friend who died in 1976 and my grandfather who died in 1979. I wanted to go to them but heard from them that "no" not yet. I was disappointed and angry as I wanted to see them, especially my mom. Then I was in a beautiful place a kind of endless sprawling landscape that was warm and sunny. I wanted to stay there and felt fantastic in that there were no more questions to be asked nor problems to overcome. All is so simple. I just knew all the answers: there was nothing other than love and service... that was it. Then I sensed something in front of me and heard a voice (thought) encourage me to look at my life. I didn't want to do that since I was enjoying my

experience, but did so anyway. I looked over my life and saw incidents that quickly showed me that there were things I had to do. I said, "I think I gotta lot of work to do" to which the reply was "well, you had better get at it." I then found myself back and awake staring at the back side of the driver's clutch pedal. I had been in the passenger seat before. I moved my feet and was relieved that my back was not broken, and then waited until the firemen smashed the back window and pulled me out of the car.

13. A severe head-on collision took three lives. I was in the front passenger's seat asleep but awoke to our vehicle lunging out of its lane. I watched the driver, a dear friend of mine for 25 years, frantically attempt to recover the vehicle amid utter shock from the lunge. Headlights wrapped around a corner at speed to face us. With an engineering background, it was clear to me that there would be four bodies in the end. ... At that moment my spirit flung out of my body, landing like a child at the chest of a much larger being. Without any hesitation I said, with a loud, deep voice and mixed tone of commitment/reason/plea, "I'm not xxx done yet." A second conscious/third being looked on in utter disbelief as if I said to myself, "Who do you think you are staying with this being and not returning to your mangled body?" ... There was no light, just a dark setting and no pain. A physical spirit—as if in my own body—renewed and I felt the landing against this other spirit

physically. I pushed away from the larger-than-life spirit and by doing so must have moved my actual arms outward simultaneously. Once back in my body ...

14. The weirdest part, however, happened as soon as I hit the bump before the car went airborne. I felt like I was floating above my right shoulder with the roof of the car a foot higher and I was against it. I saw my body, again in slow motion, like a rag doll and I remember thinking, "What the hell? Is that me? What's going on?" And just like that, it was over.

15. I was driving a small sports car which began careening across the 4-5 lanes of the one-way deck of the bridge that took (what seemed to me to be far too long to long for the vehicle to stop. The car felt as it was lifting up off the road as if it was going to "fly" into the SF Bay below. While waiting for the car to settle, my life literally flashed before me. At the time, I had a beautiful young 2-yr old daughter, who my mother was babysitting, and during that moment all I could think of was, "Oh, my God, my baby!" as I began thinking that I was going to die. Then, as if I were two people, a voice inside said "Hillari will be fine. Mama will raise her. She's good mother, and she did a wonderful job with me." I seemed to be more relaxed then. Then the thought came to me that this was taking too long. Maybe I'm not going to die. I began praying, "If I'm not going to die, Lord, please don't let me be in too much pain." Once the vehicle stopped totally, I did not

feel ANY pain—just disorientation. The next thing I knew, a Calif. Hwy patrolman opened my door and asked if I was alright.

FLOATING ONE MEANS OF MOVEMENT

1. I was floating, without a body, but still I could move around.
2. I was injured playing basketball. This is where my experience began. I was looking down on the whole schoolyard from above, as though floating in the air, and could see my fellow-players weeping and crying out.
3. I blacked out ... At this time I looked down on myself lying there with my friends around me. I could hear what they were saying and what was going on. I heard the TV and the commercials and show I was watching. I felt myself kinda floating above them near the ceiling.
4. Then I opened my eyes and I was no longer in the operating room. I seemed to be floating.
5. While being operated on I remember floating in the corner of the room above the operating table looking down at myself wondering what was going on.
6. Drowning. For a while, I ceased to exist... then darkness, a clear sensation of floating, during which my mind continued to function. I said to myself: "Ah, well, here you are then, this is death for you! It's not so bad as all that, after all.
L. [Did your vision differ in any way from your normal, everyday vision (in any aspect...)?] I could float in the air, and watch my body.

7. I had to go under general anesthesia but something went wrong. I found myself floating in above the surgery room and surprised that I seemed to have no weight at all. I was very light and movement was really easy compared to physical movement. I looked down and saw my body and the doctors working on me. I heard them yelling, "We are losing him." They struggled to get me back to life and I was so confused thinking, "Wow! Why do they bother? I don't need my body I'm fine, actually better than before."

8. As I am drifting off to sleep, my sight had a new angle, and I noticed I was laying on my back, with my arms crossed, like I was in a casket. My realization was that I saw me from a new direction, and I watched myself for a few more moments. Then I floated around the room, in the most calm manner. Now this room was becoming more than I ever could of imagined. This was fun, and something to make even the most analytical person become perplexed. It was time to go outside, and I was headed for the window. However, as I turned slowly, there was darkness, and a small light at the apparent end. In this tunnel, I could see glimpses of dark blue, purple and gold specks, illuminating the walls of this long, and very quiet tunnel. The tranquility that was within there is now capturing my entire being, and was enough for this highly anxious girl, want to stay here for a long while. As I am floating toward the light, I felt compelled to

continue this uncertain and positive experience. The light is becoming brighter and larger, and all I could feel is the presence of good, and now am for sure, this is where I need to be. Finally, the end of the tunnel is here, and I am enveloped in that same light, that without a word spoken, directed me here. It was several minutes of complete peace. There was nothing but the light. The next thing I remember is waking up two days later in ICU.

9. I only remember that when we were at the emergency room, that I was floating above my body. My body was on a stretcher or gurney and my mom was next to me crying. I remember seeing someone come up and feel my arm for a pulse (I assume this) and turning to my mother and shaking his head. [Did you experience a separation of your consciousness from your body?] I was like whole, but floating above everything. I did not seem to be solid.

10. I collapsed...drove me to the nearest hospital. I was able to hear them, but I couldn't move or talk.

I felt as though I were floating up toward the rather high ceiling. I felt a breeze on my left side, and turned to look toward that direction. I rolled over and could look down on myself, or my body, lying on the table. I remember thinking, "Wow! Nancy was right. I AM really skinny!" I weighed about 130 at the time. With my height and structure, I should weigh 145-150 or so. While I was looking down at my body, I heard a doctor say, "We're losing him!" Everything seemed to be in slow motion. I saw him pound on my chest—I suppose to re-start my heart I tried to say, "No! Don't hurt him. Leave him alone." I realized it seemed a bit strange to refer to myself as "him," but at that time, I felt that I was the entity looking down on a man who looked a lot like I used to look, but that it wasn't really me. I floated. I turned over so that I was lying (floating) on my back. The intense brightness of the hospital room started fading away and became a gentle "fog." I remember thinking it was a pale green and wondered how I knew that because I knew I had my eyes closed. I felt that I was near something wonderful and exciting but I didn't know what it was. But I was gently drifting toward it. The "nice place" whatever or wherever it was, was down and to the right. That is, if I had been lying with my head to the north and feet to the south, the place would have been southwest, or maybe south-southwest. It wasn't really "down" but toward my feet. I sensed that whatever that place was—it was brighter than the green mist. Not uncomfortably bright as the hospital had been, but comfortably bright. I wanted to go there. I did have the flash review of life. While I felt that everything was moving extremely slowly, the review was incredibly fast. I remembered a lot of incidents from the past . . . re-performed roles . . . held "conversations" with people. I remembered my entire life, almost as if I were re-living life on multiple levels simultaneously. I felt this incredible power to devote my total concentration on several different things at the same time. Suddenly I "slammed" back into my body.

11. Grandma said that she was laying in her hospital bed, when she suddenly felt like she was floating. She turned around and looked down at her body laying on the bed, then looked ahead to see a bright light and a long grassy hill. She said that her first thought was, "There is no way that I can climb that hill," before she was floating above it to wherever her destination lay. She said she could smell roses everywhere, and as she reached the crest of the hill, there were roses of every color and size. She told us that their scent was almost overwhelming, the smell was so sweet. She continued on, over the roses, and at the top of the hill there stood a crowd of people. She said that she recognized my grandfather, her mother and father, her brothers, and several other family members, but then an angel of unspeakable beauty stopped her as she headed toward them.

12. I remember flying in the air and into my body. While in the air looking below at the area of the crash site, I was floating down into my body.

13. Although this near-death experience occurred 65 years ago (1943), I will never get it out of my mind. After anesthesia I felt my body rise into the air above the surgeons and operating table, and I was looking down on this

little boy lying there with two men hovering over him.

14. The feeling of floating above all this was exciting. I had never experienced anything like it before. After briefly observing the activity beneath, my floating self began to slowly turn toward a window high on the wall in the operating room. Through this window I could see a bright light, which seemed to be beckoning to me. Fascinated, I began drifting toward the source of the light because I wanted to pass through the opening of the window and into the light. Suddenly it all disappeared and my next memory was of lying in a hospital bed.

15. Then I found myself in a blue tunnel. ... I floated gently, quite slowly along this tunnel and fully relaxed.

16. I was riding my bicycle home from high school when a driver ran a stop sign and hit me really hard and fast from the side. I flew over the vehicle and landed head first onto the pavement. I remember feeling my body float up in the air and seeing myself lying on the street surrounded by people. It felt like I was a helium balloon floating above the accident scene. I felt calm. When I noticed my school uniform skirt was up and showing my underwear, I became self-conscious and panicked! The next thing I knew, I felt my body being sucked back into my body. I then pushed my skirt down and came into consciousness.

17. I had lost consciousness and then flat lined two times. During this time, I opened my eyes and could feel something different. I was in a dark tunnel with space on each side of me. I could tell I was moving and I didn't know how. I was floating toward light shining through a crack in a door. This light was so bright that it hurt my eyes. I was going toward this light.

18. I felt a sensation of floating over the water, watching myself and not hurting or having any thoughts about being in distress. The last thing I remember is seeing how a man grabbed my hair to pull me from the water.

19. Emergency surgery. I closed my eyes for a moment. All of a sudden I was off the planet and floating way above the earth, although I could feel it behind me. I was looking into a star field— a massive, infinite entity that encompassed all of the galaxies, all of space, and some presence which is right in front of us all of the time that the earth sits in. It was massive and unimaginable. And, I had the thought that all of the dark matter and dark energy in the whole of the void was God. I was overwhelmed by the size of this presence. I understood that it knew everything about me as if it had built me cell by cell. I felt the earth behind me.

20. One morning I felt a tingling in my knees that proceeded up my legs. It was a comfortable, warm sensation. Then I noticed a strange thing— the bright sunny day I could see through the large windows had turned a beautiful deep

purple. There were little golden lights twinkling in that sky. I felt really warm and comfortable looking at that scene. Next I remember feeling myself floating up toward the ceiling. Looking down, I saw myself still in bed asleep and very far away; it was as though I was much higher up.

21. The background sky was of an inky, dark blue color and the billions of stars were beautiful. The vastness was indescribable and extremely beautiful. I appeared to be floating and was not aware that I was standing on anything. I just wanted to be there and not move. The peace was so overwhelming and so comforting.

22. The weirdest part, however, happened as soon as I hit the bump before the car went airborne. I felt like I was floating above my right shoulder with the roof of the car a foot higher and I was against it. I saw my body, again in slow motion, like a rag doll and I remember thinking, "What the hell? Is that me? What's going on?" And just like that, it was over.

23. The next thing I knew I was floating above my body and watching it as people were giving me CPR. I heard a voice that said, "Why have you worried so much in your life?" I looked at my body again. The voice said, "What good is it now?" I turned to see who was talking and the ceiling was not a barrier to me anymore. I went through to the outside and I looked in the night sky for the voice's origin. ... I then recognized the voice as it said, "Here is your assured home you built while you were living. Have you finished

everything you want in this life?" I thought about my woodcarvings that were not finished. I found myself back in my body that instant.

24. I remember walking with Jesus, but we weren't walking in the physical sense. The best way I can describe our walking is in mid-air, floating a bare spare above the ground of a beautiful garden. ... I could see the water and a bright glow surrounding it. The burbling of the water had a musical sound. The stream of water fairly sang.

25. I was now floating in a dark black tunnel. I tried to see the sides but they were as though they were not. I looked at my hands by my side and noticed that I was a golden transparent color. I had feet, toes, and fingers—the whole nine yards—all this golden transparent color.

26. Before we entered my guardian angel suddenly stopped me and said after my visit here I will have no doubt that heaven exists. So we entered thru the gates into a landscape that seemed like a massive garden of some sort. The grass was so bright, glowing with energy. I noticed we were not walking but floating above the ground. Your movement is controlled with your thoughts. I could not think of any bad thoughts as we could on earth.

27. I had an out-of-body experience where I was suddenly, in spirit only, floating stationary in a void of darkness. I could sense myself in the outline form of my body but my body wasn't there. ... I was just there floating stationary and

calling out. I didn't like it. This bothered me a lot. Then suddenly ... I woke up and saw my mother standing at the bottom of the bed.

28. [Car accident.] I began rising above the scene, still watching, but I was beginning to notice that something wasn't right. As I floated above the scene, I floated by a traffic signal that literally wasn't installed until the following week. Shortly after that I began feeling warmth radiating from the left and above me. I looked to see what the heat on my shoulder was and realized that I had no shoulder. My attention was drawn to the left and higher up where I noticed the most beautiful bright white light that I had ever seen.

29. I was out cold for a while. It was so strange, I saw myself floating away...down a tunnel with a bright light at the end. Once I hit the bright light, I looked around and I was in a large beautiful field. I saw my childhood dog running in the grass beside me, and I tried to stop, but I was floating too fast.

30. I floated along some more. The tunnel walls seemed to be made up of moving images. I was floating as in a warm salt bath and I was very comfortable. I found I could think clearly with no distractions.

31. I was at this point bodiless, formless, floating in a black warm void.

32. I distinctly remember starting to feel my body leaving my body and floating up to the top of the room as I looked down there were five doctors, three nurses, IV's being put in both arms, and a

heart machine trying to bring me back! ... The next thing I recall was floating way up to a place in a bright luminous light that I have never seen in this world. ... After that I started floating toward a tunnel. It was very long but the light on the other side was unbelievable. ... I started floating back. Next thing I remember looking down at my body with all those doctors trying to bring me back and fighting for them not to!!

33. I vividly recall floating/hovering above myself and thinking: "What am I doing up here?" I remember the room being dark as I hovered at the ceiling, looking down on myself, as I apparently slept.

34. I remember floating above my body and seeing visions of my own funeral, my parents and girlfriend were all crying over my casket. Then I was starting to leave the hospital room and ascend to another place. As if the walls of the hospital where fading away and this world was disappearing another world was simultaneously appearing to me. I felt no pain and noticed my body was not breathing or did it have a heart beat.

35. I seemed to float higher and higher when I saw a bright white light in the distance. It grew in brilliance as though I were approaching a star in a night sky, yet it didn't cause any discomfort to my eyes. At the same time I felt a pulling sensation from the light from my navel and also simultaneously I was overcome with the most

wondrous emotions of love and joy and acceptance.

36. Several post-trauma memories later came to me, such as: When I felt the car lift up, it was me. I was lifting up, possibly outside my body. Then, I began seeing myself floating through a tunnel of cloud-like fog, quite much like giant cotton balls. I saw images ahead, perhaps 7-10 individuals. They were all wearing white. (If they were robes or jumpsuits they were wearing, I couldn't tell.) Nor could I see their faces, but I did know that I was heading for a beautiful, calm place. I felt as if I knew the people ahead, and I also felt as if they were there to greet me. It felt so comfortable where I was going and I wasn't frightened. I felt a relief—then, all of a sudden, I felt and heard a kind-of big "WHOOOSH", like some great tidal wave, and the clouds were gone as abruptly as they came.

37. I felt a force pulling me slightly. I felt curious and floated with it. The environment was not hot, not cold. I felt a part of it. It was most pleasant and peaceful. ... I stopped and just floated and bobbed. the vibrations again, and again made me drift towards it with a "What's that?" thought. It was then I heard words: "BENNY! I saw her suddenly and I asked, "What do you want?" I was back.

38. In the ambulance along the way I died for a short while. I recall as what seemed to be a dream, floating in a distant corner of the ambulance watching my mother crying out, "Oh

my god! He died!" I watched the attendant working on my body. Next thing I knew I was back in my own body and I heard my mom saying, "Oh look he's back!" She cried. In the hospital, after several tests, I had died a couple more times and was revived.

39. I was in bed asleep. Suddenly I had the sensation of floating up through darkness to a bright light. When I reached the light I floated into a room that was large and sandstone colored. ... I began floating back away from them, back to where I entered the room. I had the sensation of floating down into the darkness again, back to my body.

40. I have vague, very vague recollections of looking down on a body in a bed with tubes and machines, but I cannot honestly say that it was mine. I was, well, floating is not an adequate description, more like held up, contained, buoyed, sustained in a warm, dry, medium of some sort, suspended without pressure or any feeling of containment, just there. I felt safe, warm, calm, without pain or fogginess at all, completely aware.

41. It seemed that as the scene below me faded, I must have been 40 feet above it. I seem to remember leaving the house (floated through the roof?) and a brief encounter with the blizzard, and then all sensation just vanished.

WE EXIST IN BOTH REALMS
AT THE SAME TIME

1. There is no need for any fear or anxiety as we exist here also.

2. I think a part of me is in that Light, and I've been only partly here on earth since 1973.

3. It's so apparent, yet we cannot see it while living in the form. At that very moment I likened it to an ant that could never perceive a human in its entirety, its complexity, or its completeness, yet we are right there to be seen if only the ant had the capacity.

4. There is no difference between here and there. They are here but we don't see them because we are too caught up in the physical world.

5. It is vast. I can't find the words, but there is a message which seems to give me the impression that this place is always here, and is present in all things, and beings.

6. Since my NDE, I realize that I exist in this "other place" at the same time as I exist in this physical space. There is no need for any fear or anxiety as we exist here also.

7. Just as I realized that was my lifeless body in the bed below, my thoughts were abruptly distracted.

8. All the time there was a being with me. I realized that it always had been with me!

9. I "recognized" that this entity had been with me all my life. I don't know if it was what people call a guardian angel or if it was just another disassociated aspect of my psyche. However, I

suddenly remembered that this entity had "spoken" to me many times earlier in my life.

10. As a small child I drifted freely between the realm of the spiritual and physical realm.

11. It was a very strange feeling as if I was caught in between worlds or realities.

12. I was, you could say, in two places at the same time. Part of me was in the hospital bed and part of me was walking down a long dark corridor.

13. [Did you have any sense of altered space or time?] I felt that my body was separate from my spirit and they were on two different planes of existence.

14. All the time I was also aware of my body and I was watching what was happening to it.

15. I had departed from my physical body and was looking at my hospital room from the corner of the ceiling.

16. I tried to say, "No! Don't hurt him. Leave him alone." I realized it seemed a bit strange to refer to myself as "him," but at that time, I felt that I was the entity looking down on a man who looked a lot like I used to look but that it wasn't really me.

17. The next thing I saw was my body below me. ... But to me it wasn't me because I was here above this body that was mine.

18. I found myself outside my body as a transparent and weightless me.

19. [Did you have any sense of altered space or time?] My experience consisted of becoming

consciously aware of floating above my body and observing medical personnel working frantically on my body which I could see on the ER gurney.

21. I vividly recall floating/hovering above myself and thinking: "What am I doing up here?"

22. I thought, "Hey what's going on? That's me down there?"

23. I was me looking down but was not Bob. I did not even know Bob, but I was still me as I was before I drowned.

24. I thought, "Hey what's going on? That's me down there?"

25. Just as I realized that was my lifeless body in the bed below, my thoughts were abruptly distracted.

26. I tried to say, "No! Don't hurt him. Leave him alone." I realized it seemed a bit strange to refer to myself as "him," but at that time, I felt that I was the entity looking down on a man who looked a lot like I used to look but that it wasn't really me.

27. She then explained to me that I would not see her for a while, but that she would always be with me.

28. He told me to do not cry any more for him, that he died because it was his time and that he was taking care of me from that dimension.

29. [Did you have any sense of altered space or time?] I was definitely in two places at the same time.

VOIDS

1. [Drowning] I could clearly feel/see that the wind still blew, the water still lapped around me, the sun continued to shine bright and strong. I could feel these elements but they did not affect the void time/space that was created around me. At the end, I made a decision and at that point, the "void" stopped and, with difficulty, I made it back to the shore

2. There are doors sliding in front of me, each door representing a stage of my past life since childhood, and one door representing present day. Somehow I knew I had to enter the right door in the limited time I had as after that all the doors would close never to open again leaving me all alone in the dark void forever. I also knew that if I entered the wrong door the memories from that stage of my life till today would be erased. I started fearing not death but isolation or never being able to see my two sons & husband again, or even not recognizing them after I wake up. I feel time is slipping out of my hands and I decide that I'd rather enter the wrong door than stay back in my head.

3. [Was the kind of experience difficult to express in words?] It was hard to believe by others as I saw myself or felt I was walking around outside of the car, but also experienced being highly conscious in a dark void, but I was not afraid. Although it was dark, I felt I could see. There was no up, down or sideways ... no sense of direction.

I was alone. Apparently the Buddhists call this Bardo. ... [Did you see a light?] I saw light when I experienced being outside of the car and darkness, pitch black darkness in the void

4. I was in a dark void or space like in the universe without the stars. In the distance was a light, no definite shape, similar to a puddle of spilled water. The light was pulsating as if alive. I began to move toward the light, was being drawn, all of a sudden it was like I was moving at the speed of light.

5. [Suicide Attempt] Am I going to be here in this place forever! This abyss! What have I done! The fear was off the charts. We are not supposed to take our own life. I was fully aware of what I had done and the thought of being alone in that nothing forever was unbearable but what could I do? It was too late. Suddenly in the void I heard a voice, a male voice, and He said, "It's o.k. It's all right. It's all good." I went from total terror to total peace and acceptance of my life and responsibility. I was no longer worried about heaven or hell or my death. This voice accepted me, and did not judge me. I in a way had judged myself and clearly had an instant understanding of my life. And how important it is to play our lives out to the end regardless of how hard it is. And to get off of ourselves and to be in the company of each other to help each other. That abyss was total separation from all.

6. I remember being in a dark grey void. A voice said to me: "Richard, why are you here?" I said: "I

want to come home." The voice replied: "It's not time yet. You have more work to do. You have a family that loves you and that you need to take care of."

7. Suddenly in the void I heard a voice, a male voice, and He said, "It's o.k. It's all right. It's all good." I went from total terror to total peace and acceptance of my life and responsibility. I was no longer worried about heaven or hell or my death.

8. I was in an atmosphere of absolute white that had no ending anywhere. It was an unending white void. Suddenly, my late parents came to greet me but I do not recall them speaking to me. Other people were there suddenly and I did not recognize any of them. I was at total peace and comfort.

9. I saw a black void endless in depth. I remember just thinking, "Hmm, okay, big black void?" As I was floating in the void I turned to see what was pulling me forward slowly. I didn't feel any force on me just the sensation of being pulled towards something. I looked forward if you call it forward and saw a light in the void. I would say it was about 400 yards ahead of me and I would be there in about two minutes, at my constant speed. As I drifted towards the white light that twinkled like a star, it didn't hurt to look at it. After the year I finally realized the passage in the Bible, I believe it goes: "As I enter into the valley of the shadow of death I fear no evil." Suddenly and quickly faster than I enter the void, everything went into reverse and I moved away

from the white light. Colors that were blocks of color began to focus again and I saw the trees and house clearly again. I was back in my body in the backyard.

10. I felt more of a void of everything, emotionally and physically. I remember thinking it was nice to have no worries, no pain, fear etc. But I also noticed no joy, pleasure or any of the good counterparts. I was VERY surprised to learn that I liked the void. ... The next thing I remember is being in a void. I couldn't tell whether I was in light or darkness. I just remember NOTHING being all around me

11. While at the hospital ashore, my heart stopped again and I went to a gray void area and was looking around into the darkness. A lighted doorway appeared or beckoned me from my distant right. Above and around the door was a moving ghostly white fog (Holy Ghost?)

12. I was speeding through a black tunnel with reddish colors—so fast. I felt scared. I had no control, and the experience was horrible. It ended and I find myself in a place of black. A void. Time went on forever, but there was no time. Space went on forever, but there was no space. Time and space were one. Time and space did not exist. I felt scared. I called out. I realized there was no way out. I prayed.

13. The next thing I was sitting cross- legged (supported mid air) in the middle of a great void. It wasn't dark. It wasn't light. It was NOTHING. I was in the middle of absolutely nothing. I can't

express how empty it was. I felt no emotion. Not even calm. I seemed to be there an eternity, as if there was no such thing as time. I had been there for the whole of existence, in both directions. I knew there was something important I was supposed to be thinking about, but it was hard to care. I remembered briefly, how hard it was to breathe and whether the attached feelings meant anything. I spent some time thinking about the life that went with those feelings.

... (That is now my idea of heaven and hell. My own personal measure of how I went.) Then there was pain. And the loud voices, and I knew I was back.

14. I had an out-of-body experience where I was suddenly, in spirit only, floating stationary in a void of darkness. I could sense myself in the outline form of my body but my body wasn't there. I could see like there wasn't darkness just like a person can see when there is light in a room, but everything is black. It was extremely soundless in this space. So soundless that it actually hurt my ears not to hear sounds. No light was present. Yet, I could see clearly all around the black space just like

being in a space that had light. I knew there were invisible boundaries that I could not go through. I just knew they were there. I called out, "Isn't anyone there?" I did this several times and started to get upset. No one answered. I knew I was the only one there. I thought I was going to be alone like this forever. I was feeling extreme emotional anxiety because no one would answer me and no one was there with me. I was just there floating stationary and calling out. I didn't like it. This bothered me a lot. Then suddenly ... I woke up and saw my mother standing at the bottom of the bed.

15. I have never felt such intense fear in my life. I have no visual memory as this is happening. It's as if I was in a dark void. I have no recollection of having any type of form, just thought. Then a calming voice communicated into my mind the thought, "Yes, but it's okay."

16. I suddenly found myself in a black void. I felt very comfortable but very surprised. There was no sense of vision, including no colour or light (not even a hint of visual stimuli as one may see even when eyelids shut in a dark room), complete silence—except for the hint of a memory of a "click" having come from the left side just some moments previously, no sense of temperature or pain or touch or smell/taste whatsoever. There was a sense of enclosed space, like this black void was within a container that was not very large. There may have been a sense of being suspended—of floating but not moving— or there may have been complete stillness—at this stage of writing I cannot be sure which. There were full powers of logical reasoning and language. I found myself thinking, "Where am I? What's happened? What was I doing? ... But as my experience showed me, I was not "fully" unconscious. I was thinking quite

lucidly, even though I was unclear who or where I was—although may have soon worked that out, being disorientated initially by the sudden shock of being suspended in blackness, as my reasoning seemed very clear and sound at the time.

17. I had an experience that I know was real, not a dream. I found myself in what seemed to be a huge cavern, probably what you would consider to be a void. ... I did not feel afraid, just very alone

18. At this point, the voice, no longer audible but what I'd call telepathic, instructed me to concentrate on a fuzzy red line in a black void. As long as I concentrated on this flickering red line I'd maintain a foothold to life. I was at this point bodiless, formless, floating in a black warm void. ... I felt I was in a "waiting room" of sorts, neither in life nor death, or maybe in between. I was aware that it was my choice to go to one side or the other ... In other words, though I had no desire to return to my desiccated, disease-wracked body, I really had no choice in the practical sense—it was the only sensible option to return.

19. There was just the most horrible blackness, a void. ... I was then transported back in time to a point in the wreck where I had made a decision about saving myself or dying. This time I made the decision to live and was impelled to take a different action, which proved to be what saved my life.

20. I also knew that if I entered the wrong door the memories from that stage of my life till today

would be erased. I started fearing not death but isolation or never being able to see my two sons & husband again, or even not recognizing them after I wake up. I feel time is slipping out of my hands and I decide that I'd rather enter the wrong door than stay back in my head. ... I just think of GOD & put my foot forward to enter the speeding doors and at that very moment I feel the anesthetist slapping my cheeks & calling my name. The surgeon says SHE IS BACK.

21. It was completely black. I had no sense of a body. I was very confused. I explain it as the feeling you get if you're very little and you lose your mom in a crowd. It was total fear and aloneness. For a second thought I might be in hell, it was so empty. Then a PEACE came over me. I felt like I was totally loved, totally happy. I had no fears or worries or pains. It was wonderful. I started hearing music. Beautiful music and, I started seeing a mirage of colors.

22. Then my husband came to mind and I felt an urgency not to enjoy this void too much, that I needed to be with him and not leave him. Then I became frightened and tried to call out to him, but I thought he couldn't hear me. In my mind I was screaming a little louder and louder each time. When I thought I screamed the loudest out of panic, I finally heard me whispering to him and I realized I hadn't been heard at all. Then I guess I gave up trying to make him hear me.

23. Everything went dark, but then immediately it turned in to a vast place with no dimensions,

time or sound. I was alone in this place, or I thought I was at the time. I could still see and looked in all directions, even under myself and saw only light gray.

24. The "Void" Experiences. I fell into an altered state and found myself traveling into a dark Void. Within this Void, there was only me and I was God. There was no "other." The darkness surrounding me was absolute, and yet it was not empty. The Void seemed pregnant with probability as if every event that ever was or ever will be was contained within it. I found the experience to be completely acceptable while I was in the Void. I had no emotion or fear. Only being and knowing. Afterwards, however, when I emerged, I was overwhelmed. I cried for three days because there was no other, and I desperately wanted there to be other.

25. I was then inside some sort of dark place that was getting darker and darker. It started whirling around me, and I was feeling intense vibration inside my body. It was so powerful that I thought I was going to be dissolved. Just when it got so powerful I thought I was a goner. I was out of the "tunnel," if that is what you can call it. I was in a place of total darkness. I raised my hand and looked at it. I thought, "Almost too dark to see your hand in front of your face. What is this place?" I looked around, and I seemed to be standing on something solid, but I couldn't see it. I felt my body, and I was wearing clothes, but they seemed to be of a much finer fabric than my

tee shirt and blue jeans. ... It was bright and light, but I could see past this a dark blackness. I knew it was infinity out there.

26. I was moving head first through a dark maelstrom of what looked like black boiling clouds, feeling that I was being beckoned to the sides which frightened me.

27. I was suddenly, in spirit only, in a void of darkness. ... It was extremely soundless in this space. So soundless that it actually hurt my ears not to hear sounds. No light was present. Yet, I could see clearly all around the black space just like being in a space that had light. I knew there were invisible boundaries that I could not go through. I just knew they were there. I called out, "Isn't anyone there?" I did this several times and started to get upset. No one answered. I knew I was the only one there. I thought I was going to be alone like this forever. I was feeling extreme emotional anxiety because no one would answer me and no one was there with me. I was just there floating stationary and calling out. I didn't like it. This bothered me a lot. Then suddenly ... I woke up and saw my mother standing at the bottom of the bed.

28. Am I going to be here in this place forever! This abyss! What have I done! The fear was off the charts. We are not supposed to take our own life. I was fully aware of what I had done and the thought of being alone in that nothing forever was unbearable but what could I do? It was too late. Suddenly in the void I heard a voice, a male

voice, and He said, "It's o.k. It's all right. It's all good."

29 Then the blackest black... nothingness...I saw no tunnel, no light. Just blackness. It didn't inspire fear. I felt perfectly fine, and somewhat like a detached observer.

DARK TUNNELS

1. I felt as if I was squeezed through a dark tube of some kind. I imagine birth could be like it. It felt heavy and hard to squeeze through. When I was out of this dark tube I felt great. ... I begged to stay and then I felt this dark tight tube around me again and at this moment I heard the nurse call my name.

2. Then all of a sudden I was pulled through this tunnel to a white light.

3. I turned slowly, there was darkness, and a small light at the apparent end. In this tunnel, I could see glimpses of dark blue, purple and gold specks, illuminating the walls of this long, and very quiet tunnel. ... At that time, I turned around, back to the direction I had so calmly came from, and was immediately pulled back through the dark tunnel. It was so fast, that I didn't see any of the magical colors within the dark travel.

4. I became aware that I was traveling rapidly through darkness. It wasn't quite a tunnel, but it did seem to have a form and direction, even though it was dark. ... I got closer to the light, to the point where the darkness disappeared and I was preparing to join the light.

5. Next thing I remember was complete darkness and feeling very confused. Then I realized I was in a tunnel and did not know how to get out. I started to feel scared and it was then that I saw a glow of light and a hand reach out to me. [Did you pass into or through a tunnel or enclosure?]

The tunnel was the only thing I did not like. It was very dark and you are just walking until you see the light.

6. I travel in a black tunnel...with great speed... forgotten everything....in this world.

7. Next was the tunnel. It was a black tunnel through a blacker sky littered with stars off in the distance. The tunnel turned and twisted like a waterslide and we went for a long time. After a time, I just kind of plopped out at the other end with two really washed out watercolor images of me.

8. I just remember going into a wide and long tunnel, like entering a train tunnel. At the beginning there was still earthly light, then I entered darkness which was not complete even as it was getting denser and denser, and it filled the whole arch, darkness was indeed not black but rather dark grey and thick in its outlines, dense, in the center the void was clear. At the end of this tunnel, I saw this beautiful, extremely attractive light, and to which I came closer very fast.

9. Suddenly I entered a dark tunnel, feeling all the time at peace and in harmony, feeling wonderful

10. I remember a loud roaring in my ears and rushing through a long, dark tunnel at the end of which was a very bright light. 11. Behind me was a dark tunnel with a light at the end. 12. The tunnel that everybody talks about isn't horizontal, but vertical, as if you were in a dark well and then you begin to go upwards as if you

were being drawn from above. And at the apex of the tunnel, you are filled with a very bright light.

13. Normally the thought of a tunnel would scare me, because I'm highly claustrophobic, but this tunnel was part of me and I was happy. Nothing was separate.

14. I did move through a black, velvety tunnel, a color black I had never seen nor can I describe, toward a very distant pinpoint of light.

15. I made a breath-taking dive into a tunnel. I saw motionless people. I saw old colleagues deceased since many years, making signs: "Come along with us." I also saw my parents, deceased in 1979, making signs in order to invite me to follow them.

15. I was drawn through a tunnel toward a bright light. There were other lights along the tunnel that were people. I also saw a woman who might be me grown up. [Did you pass into or through a tunnel or enclosure?] It was a tunnel that was dark with lights that were people...at the end was an incredible bright light.

16. [Did you see a light?] It seemed the farther down the tunnel I went the farther from the light I got, until it was void of light and reached the end.

17. Went into tunnel. It was black.

18. After a bit the ceiling dissolved into darkness and opened up. I was drawn upward into a sort of tunnel although I could not see the walls. ... I was escorted back to the dark cave and I returned down the tunnel, with air rushing by, as

on the way up.

19. Everything became dark and suddenly I was falling through a tunnel. It looked very futuristic, like something out of Star Wars, with lights zooming by me at warp speed.

20. I was speeding through a black tunnel with reddish colors—so fast. I felt scared. I had no control, and the experience was horrible. It ended and I find myself in a place of black. A void. Time went on forever, but there was no time. Space went on forever, but there was no space. Time and space were one. Time and space did not exist.

21. Suddenly I would be "sucked" into a black tunnel. Each time I was in a sitting position and traveling backwards at what seemed to be incredible speed.

22. Suddenly, I was pulled into complete darkness. Amidst the total darkness, I smelled an indescribable odor. ... Then I began to feel myself moving upward. As I was being pulled upward, I began to feel as if I was in a tunnel, an endless, pitch-black tunnel.

23. I felt like I was going down a tunnel. It was dark at first and then it was very light, bright sun light.

24. I felt distinctness in the tunnel with the outer darkness being a void.

25. I saw a spherical long dark tunnel before my eyes, spinning around me, full of what seemed to be dark clouds.

26. I remember a black tunnel and being totally

out. ... This place had no planets or stars; there was darkness and the only light source was the light humanoid beings.

27. She and the wolf led me down a long dark tunnel. ... The woman and the wolf were there and walked me back through the tunnel.

28. I was in a dark tunnel with space on each side of me. I could tell I was moving and I didn't know how.

29. I began a terrifying journey down a black spiral tunnel to an amazingly bright light, the likes I have never seen before or since. ... The journey back was the same, but this time into darkness.

30. I entered a dark channel, a corridor, a tunnel, a canal... I remember thinking, "Yes, this is the birth canal." I thought with a big sigh, "I don't want to be born again." I realized with relief that wasn't happening.

31. I was standing in a dimly lit long tunnel and began walking toward the source of the light. 32. I was now floating in a dark black tunnel. I tried to see the sides but they were as though they were not. I looked at my hands by my side and noticed that I was a golden transparent color. I had feet, toes, and fingers—the whole nine yards—all this golden transparent color. I looked ahead of me and saw a distant light, a dot of light very far away and blurry. I squinted to try to focus, but I was suddenly outside the tube in a vast flat, black darkness of space. I looked for stars but saw only the dark rubbery looking tube

stretching ahead of me into forever. Not in a straight line either. That confused me because when you look into a hose you need to stretch it out in order to see the light at the other end. Now, here's something that is hard to explain. I was watching myself inside the tunnel at the same time I was looking at myself outside the tunnel, all seeing and all questions happening at the same time. How could I be down in that tunnel seeing a light at the end of it when I'm floating out here seeing a tunnel that is not in a straight line? Suddenly, I was thrust at a high rate of speed through the tunnel toward the light. ... Suddenly I was in darkness and yelling "No!!!!" I woke up.

33. I remember leaving the scene - moving up a dark tunnel - being pulled slowly by my shoulders.

34. I went through a long dark tunnel toward a bright light.

35. I began to move in what I'll call a tunnel through dark space slowly, on an angle, not straight up. I was not happy with this and afraid! As I ascended in this tunnel, it became warmer and I began to relax.

36. I drifted up and into a long tunnel. At first, I felt pain and sorrow. I felt, from the perspective of all those affected by me, any hurt I had caused them. It was horrible but I was forced to understand my negative influence on them. It was incredibly enlightening. I would call it purgatory and I'm glad I didn't have to stay long!

Then I floated along some more. The tunnel walls seemed to be made up of moving images. I was floating as in a warm salt bath and I was very comfortable. I found I could think clearly with no distractions.

37. After that I started floating toward a tunnel. It was very long but the light on the other side was unbelievable.

38. I immediately found myself standing in a vertical tunnel. It was dark or gray but there was a rush of brilliant white fog rushing upward through the tunnel as if it was vacuum.

39. It was then that I felt like I was in a tunnel of see sort. At the end of this tunnel the light was unbearable at first. However, I soon adjusted to the light and it was then that my "escorts" disappeared. ... I was standing on the edge of the tunnel. I looked down and saw a beautiful blue-green river. Suddenly I heard a familiar voice, "Go back Debbie, it's not your time yet!"

40. I have subsequently read others' references to a tunnel, and indeed it was like that because after a while I saw a tiny little pinprick of light which grew bigger as if I were fast approaching a faraway exit. 39. This door looked to open into a very long tunnel of light, a corridor to India-land, a tunnel, like in the "2001" movie! This amazing dream ended as I was pushed into this tunnel and pushed so that I was moving at a very high speed. BUT I could see, on my right, a forest of trees! I flew passed them. I tried to make sure that I did not touch even a single leaf! (I learned

later that this forest is one's "FOREST OF MEMORY" ... I flew off at high speed to India-land, but there was a hint given me at the very last moment of the vision-awareness, that the "Younger Center" and the tunnel to India-land were CREATED and maintained by some VERY high spirits from the CELESTIAL level of the heavens, the GOD realms where LOVE is the way, and where ALL the progressive "heaven-ladders-to-ascend-to-higher-being-ness are created and operated. I actually SENSED a presence of a GREAT SPIRIT FORM over the top of this whole tunnel, directing it. I gather from this that all of the lower heavens are created and maintained by high spirits and Angels and Emissaries of the Lord himself—by INFERENCE our lives here on earth are likewise SUPPORTED and upheld by Guides—Angels—and other God-enfranchised beings. The human race and YOU, READER OF THIS VISION, are in Very Good Hands!!!!

41. During her coma, she also saw her body while sitting in a "chair" with a long tunnel above her. Needless to say, she didn't go in. She does not know why.

COLORS: MISCELLANIOUS

1. I also remember wandering around in a charcoal-colored fog.

2. I remember seeing a brightly colored dome, spires, and living a whole life someplace else.

3. Then she saw IT, the music and colors that were indescribably beautiful.

4. There was a figure off to the left side of this door. To me it looked transparent, the color of liquid coffee held up to the light.

5. I was instantly surrounded by the most beautiful, pure light and colors that cannot even be imagined.

6. I would say LIGHT AND EVEN SHADOW might (?) look like what nuclear physics can produce: light is made of small ultra bright dots, hyper mobiles and DENSE, energy. Colors are very, very vivid, clear, as if PURE, and each light dot that makes up the light seems to be individual, but it participates to the whole that constitutes the light, and it seems to contain the whole color prism.

7. All around me were beings of pulsing, colored light, and indescribable music/singing full of joy and praise.

8. The 'many who were there' were without any body-form like we know, they merely looked like little packets or little dull colored balls.

9. The being of light—I lack a better description—began to look through my life. It

simply shone into me and scenes from my life projected around me as if I were seeing them again. A lot like looking at a hologram, but full color 3D with sound and scent.

10. I don't know what color the door was, all I knew was it was a door and I was not going through it!

11. Colors that were blocks of color began to focus again and I saw the trees and house clearly again. I was back in my body in the backyard.

12. I turned slowly, there was darkness, and a small light at the apparent end. In this tunnel, I could see glimpses of dark blue, purple and gold specks, illuminating the walls of this long, and very quiet tunnel. ... At that time, I turned around, back to the direction I had so calmly came from, and was immediately pulled back through the dark tunnel. It was so fast, that I didn't see any of the magical colors within the dark travel.

13. I saw colors that seem to mix together in glimmery iridescence. It was pure joy and happiness. It felt more real than anything I've experienced on earth.

14. I was walking into the city. It was gold and just cast off all the light in this world. There was no sun or moon but the sky was so beautiful. There was colors of all kinds.

15. There was a river and a pure golden bridge that crossed over it. In the distance I saw a city with towers all in gold and white and amazing bright colors.

16. It was wonderful. I started hearing music.

Beautiful music and, I started seeing a mirage of colors.

17. Then everything went white, not exactly white, but colorless.

DATA SUMMARIES

THIRTY-TWO RELIABLE AFTERLIFE DETAILS

"She said to me: 'This is what it will
be like when you come here'."

Dear Reader:

Here are the 32 details presented in five different ways, one way in each appendix, so that we might better comprehend our existence after life.

-SELF-

Indescribable Peace
Thinking Continues
Extreme Vision
Regain Vast Knowledge
Consciousness Continues

-ENVIRONS-

Interaction with Other Persons
Time
Space
Mind-to-Mind Communication
Afterlife Is Home
Deceased Family Members
Accompanied by Guide
Light Beings

Persons with No Gender
Persons Shaped Like Orbs
Dark Tunnels
Love from the Guide
White
Into the Light and Beyond
White Clothing
Used Term "Guide"
Blue
Music
Blue-White
Punishment Places
Rules and Enforcement
Pets

-PHYSICAL LIFE-

Willing Return to Life After Visit
Mission to Accomplish
Past and Future Lives Seen
Guides Intervene?
Exist in Both Realms At Same Time

EXPANDED DETAILS OF OUR EXISTENCE AFTER LIFE

We are here to love each other and learn. We will return "Home," referring to where we are before and after physical life. Physical life is a sojourn, a short residence away from home.

Once we leave our bodies in order to return to the other realm, our consciousness and thinking continue and become more powerful.

We have a mission to complete in life. For many it is for the for the purpose of personal growth.

The afterlife is inhabited by persons.

On our way to the light, the persons we see and meet will be strangers to us. But in some cases the stranger will know us somehow.

We will communicate with other persons mind-to-mind.

Many of us will be accompanied by someone.

Some of us will refer to our accompanier as a "guide."

Our guide will be a stranger, but in some cases will somehow know us.

Many of us will feel love from our guide.

Most of us will not want to return to physical life.

The guide often is the person sending us back.

We may encounter one or more of our deceased family members and friends. They can appear to others as they wish. Many will appear as they did in their prime.

Seeing will be extremely clear and vivid. Wrote one visitor: "It was like I was seeing the world for the first time with my own true eyes. It was the equivalent of taking off a pair of foggy ski-goggles or glasses."

We will be able to see clearly in the dark.

We will be able to see from more than one point of view at the same time.

We will see in all directions, 360 degrees.

Some of us will view past and/or future lives.

Perhaps we exist in both realms at the same time.

We will regain vast knowledge. We will forget our vast knowledge if we return to physical life.

Many of us will experience indescribable peace.

There is space and time in the afterlife. That is because the mind structures experience with space and time.

Many of us will experience music.

Prominent colors: white the most frequently mentioned by far, followed by blue and then a blue-white combination.

Possibly guides intervene in physical life.
Some of us will go into, and some even beyond, the light.

Some will go into and beyond the light.

Rules and enforcement exist there.

You might see persons with no apparent gender and persons shaped like orbs.

Projected Number of Visitors (±5%) Reporting Each
Afterlife Detail in the Online Archives Sampled
(N=20,000)

-

SELF-

Indescribable Peace 6,000
Thinking Continued 3,174
Regained Vast Knowledge 2,652
Love 2,100 (approx.)
Extreme Vision 2,097
Consciousness Continued 1,435

-OTHER PERSONS-

Spoke of Persons 15,000+
Guides 3,261
Mind-to-Mind Communication 3,044
Deceased Family and Friends Seen 2,348
Love from the Guide 1,522
Used Term "Guide" 783
Persons Shaped Like Orbs 478
Persons with No Apparent Gender 347

-ENVIRONS-

Used Time Terms 15,000+
Used Space Terms 15,000+
Dark Tunnels 1,783

-PHYSICAL LIFE-

Number of Reports in the Random Sample
(n = 460) for Each Afterlife Detail

-SELF-

Indescribable Peace 138
Thinking Continued 73
Regained Vast Knowledge 61
Extremely Powerful Vision 48
Consciousness Continued 33

-OTHER PERSONS-

Spoke of Persons 300+
Guides 75
Mind-to-Mind Communication 70
Deceased Family and Friends Seen 54
Love from the Guide 35
Used Term "Guide" 18
Persons Shaped Like Orbs 11
Persons with No Apparent Gender 8

-Appendix E-

Ranking by Projected Number of Visitors Reporting Each
Afterlife Detail (in Descending Order)
Space and Time There
Indescribable Peace
Guides
Thinking Continued
Mind-to-Mind Communication
Regained Vast Knowledge
Extreme Vision
Deceased Family Members Seen
Rules and Enforcement
Dark Tunnels
Home
Love from the Guide
Consciousness Continued
A Mission to Accomplish in Life
White Color
Exist in Both Realms At Same Time
Voids
Into the Light and Beyond
White Clothing
Used Term "Guide"
Willing Return to Life After Visit
Past and Future Lives Seen
Color Blue
Music
Guides Intervene in Physical Life?
Blue-White Color Combination
Punishment Places
Persons with No Apparent Gender
Persons Shaped Like Orbs
Pets

Percentage of Activities Participated in by Visitors to YACHEP National Park, Western Australia, 42 Kilometres North of Perth.	
Sightseeing 65.0	Rest/relax 12.0
Bird/wildlife viewing 60.0	See the sights 8.0
Relaxing/fun/enjoyment 52.0	Fitness/health 7.0
Enjoy nature/outdoors 33	Recreational activities 2.0
Photography 31.0	Learn about culture 1.0
Bushwalking/hiking 28.0	Cycling 1.0
Picnicking/BBQ 27.0	Camping 1.0
Guided tours 27.0	Exercise 1.0
Break from city life 21.0	Canoeing/boating 1.0
Aboriginal/cultural sites 17.0	Swimming 0.5
Time with family/friends 16.0	Rock climbing 0.5
Learn about flora/fauna 13.0	Fishing 0.0
Other 12.0	Snorkelling / diving 0.0

[Note: Percentages add up to more than 100% due to visitor participation in more than one activity.]

Activities

Respondents were provided a list and asked, "In which of the following activities did you

or someone in your group participate while on this State Park visit?" Table 7 summarizes

the information which include some other "write in" responses. It is noticeable that:

- Activities such as hiking/biking, fishing, and canoeing/kayaking were reported
  considerably more by overnight visitors.

- Picnicking was more apt to be associated with day visitors.

- Swimming was an activity reported with almost equal frequency by both day and
  overnight visitors.

Table 7
Visitor Activities

Activity	All (n=469)	Day (n=278)	Overnight (n=185)
Swimming	59.7	57.2	63.2
Picnicking	47.8	54.3	37.8
Hiking	40.9	32.4	55.1
Overnight Camping	40.1	-	96.2
Canoe/Kayaking	22.4	9.7	42.2
Biking	14.5	6.1	27.0
Fishing	6.6	2.5	13.0
Motorized Boating	6.0	4.0	9.2
Walking (beach, etc.)	5.1	7.2	2.2
Lounging/Relaxing	1.5	2.2	0.5
Sightseeing	1.5	1.8	1.1
Sunning/Tanning	1.1	1.8	-
Other	7.5	7.6	7.6

Note: Percentages add to more than 100% due to multiple mentions

List Table

GENERAL FINDING OF THIS BOOK
The fact that hundreds, and even thousands, of afterlife visitors *independently* reported similar details forces us to conclude those details must reliably describe existence after life.

www.ingramcontent.com/pod-product-compliance
Lightning Source LLC
LaVergne TN
LVHW011342080426
835511LV00005B/106